Seeking Ghosts In
The Warwick Valley

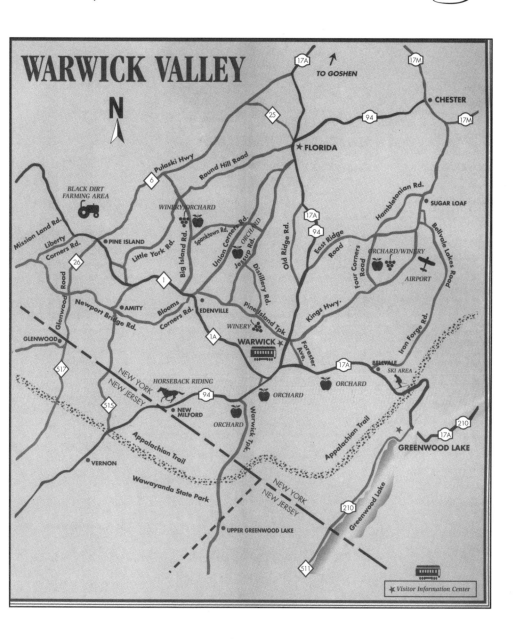

WARWICK VALLEY

N

TO GOSHEN

17A · 17M

CHESTER

25 · 94 · 17M

FLORIDA

Pulaski Hwy · Round Hill Road

6

BLACK DIRT FARMING AREA

WINERY/ORCHARD

Hambletonian Rd.

SUGAR LOAF

17A · 94

Mission Land Rd. · Liberty Corners Rd.

PINE ISLAND

Little York Rd. · Big Island Rd. · Spanktown Rd. · Union Corners Rd. · Jessup Rd. · ORCHARD

Old Ridge Rd.

East Ridge Road · Four Corners Road

ORCHARD/WINERY

Bellvale Lakes Road

AIRPORT

26

Glenwood Road

Newport Bridge Rd. · AMITY · Blooms Corners Rd. · EDENVILLE

1

Distillery Rd. · Pine Island Tpk.

Kings Hwy.

Iron Forge Rd.

WINERY

1A

WARWICK

Forester Ave.

17A

BELLVALE SKI AREA

GLENWOOD

517

NEW YORK NEW JERSEY

HORSEBACK RIDING

94

ORCHARD · ORCHARD

515

NEW MILFORD

ORCHARD

Warwick Tpk.

Appalachian Trail

210 · 17A

GREENWOOD LAKE

VERNON

Appalachian Trail

Wawayanda State Park

NEW YORK NEW JERSEY

Greenwood Lake

210

UPPER GREENWOOD LAKE

511

★ Visitor Information Center

WARWICK

Schiffer Publishing Ltd ®

4880 Lower Valley Road, Atglen, PA 19310 USA

Seeking Ghosts In The Warwick Valley

60 Personal Accounts

Donna Reis

Designed by Bonnie M. Hensley
Cover design by Bruce M. Waters
Type set in Martisse/ZapfChan Dm BT

ISBN: 0-7643-1740-7
Printed in China

Published by Schiffer Publishing Ltd.
4880 Lower Valley Road
Atglen, PA 19310
Phone: (610) 593-1777; Fax: (610) 593-2002
E-mail: Schifferbk@aol.com
Please visit our web site catalog at
www.schifferbooks.com

This book may be purchased from the publisher.
Include $3.95 for shipping. Please try your bookstore first.
We are always looking for people to write books on new and related subjects. If you
have an idea for a book please contact us at the above address.
You may write for a free catalog.

In Europe, Schiffer books are distributed by
Bushwood Books
6 Marksbury Avenue
Kew Gardens
Surrey TW9 4JF England
Phone: 44 (0) 20-8392-8585; Fax: 44 (0) 20-8392-9876
E-mail: Bushwd@aol.com
Free postage in the UK. Europe: air mail at cost.

DEDICATION

For Jimmy

"There are so many spirits in Warwick that a séance will only stir them up. And then who knows what will happen!" — unknown

Boo!
Donna Lewis

CONTENTS

ACKNOWLEDGMENTS

Grateful acknowledgment is given to the magazines and newspapers in which many of these stories first appeared, often in slightly different form.

Hudson Valley: Surrealist Secret
The Times Herald Record: The Demarest House's Resident Trickster; Mr. Hartwick; My Father's Calling Card; The Visit
The Warwick Advertiser: My Tale; Robert

I want to give special thanks to all the people who shared their ghostly experiences with me, especially to those who were willing to confide their story, but asked that I please not put it in print, and to those who asked that I not reveal their names for the risk they took and the trust they placed in me.

I also want to thank my dear friends Kathy Romano who edited my work evening after evening for over five years and generously offered her suggestions; Shotsie Gorman, who surprised me with the amazing painting for my birthday, which is now the cover, and Christine Cole, whose pen and inks add a haunting spice to the collection. And a special thanks to Herb Hadad, who listened to several of these stories back when I first began this project and never tired of giving me his professional comments.

And most of all I want to thank my dearest husband Jimmy, who would have preferred that I spent the hours on this book with him, but never complained and always dropped everything to listen to a revision.

FOREWORD

It has been said that, from the beginning of history, all the deeds of men are recorded in the ether as if on an endless loop of video tape. It is uncertain why some people are born with special sensitivity to view and hear the events from the past when others cannot. But some of the greatest scientific minds, Einstein, Nikola Tesla, Joseph Rhodes Buchanan, had no difficulty understanding the phenomena of ghosts and spectral beings. They simply are, and have always been, part of our universe, our consciousness, our daily lives, whether we acknowledge them or not.

Donna Reis has done an outstanding and compelling job of recording some of the more intriguing tales of celestial spirits who have chosen to carry on their otherworldly lives in the beautiful Warwick Valley of Orange County, New York.

Monica Randall
Author of *Phantoms of the Hudson Valley*
The Overlook Press, New York, New York

INTRODUCTION

As leaves blaze from the Hudson Valley's rolling hills and jack-o-lanterns begin to peer from windows and doorways, I hanker after a juicy ghost story, a good scare. Why do believers and non-believers, alike, love a haunting tale? Is it because they bring back the hair-raising stories that kept us awake as children? Or that we enjoy being scared when we know we are not in danger? Or is it that they imply that perhaps death is not an end, but a transformation? Whatever it might be, ghost stories are always lots of fun and ripe for the telling.

Inspired by Halloween articles in local newspapers and magazines, I sought to raise the otherworldly beings that are believed to lurk in the valley where I live, Warwick, New York. The valley spans one hundred and four square miles and includes three villages, Florida, Greenwood Lake and Warwick and five hamlets, Amity, Bellvale, Edenville New Milford, and Pine Island. I included Sugar Loaf, also, which historically was considered one of the valley's hamlets until 1845. I began my research by taking out an ad in my local newspaper. It read, "Seeking Ghosts in the Warwick Valley. Historical and Personal Accounts Wanted." Dozens of people responded. And in case you're wondering, none seemed weird or crazy. Each telephone interview led to more stories and personal interviews. After hearing so many experiences, one might think every old house in the Warwick Valley is haunted. And even some new.

During my research, I discovered that those who encountered ghosts fell into two categories. The first type, the skeptics, were usually conservative thinkers, not believers by nature, who might even scoff at the idea of the supernatural. After experiencing a barrage of inexplicable occurrences in their homes such as footsteps heard at night on the stairs and rocking chairs that rocked without occupants, they resisted the idea of being haunted until they ran out of rational explanations such as warped floors, settling foundations, the wind. Then, a ghost became a private consideration. These people might joke about their resident spectral beings with family members, but they were reluctant to share their secrets, lest other people think they were crazy. Some were willing to tell me about the phenomena, but asked that I not print their stories or repeat them to anyone else. Others gave me permission to use their stories, but asked that I not use their real names or addresses.

The second type were born believers. Instead of beginning their interview with, "I never believed in ghosts, but, …," they began by saying, "I've always been sensitive to this sort of thing." These people are intrigued by the ghostly goings-on in their homes and hoped that I'd be as amazed by their experiences as they were. This category had a subgroup. The people in this group, although certain they had ghosts, either chose to keep their stories to themselves or told them in church-like voices and asked that I not include them in the book out of respect for the spirits themselves. In such cases, the homeowner had come to think of his ghost or ghosts as members of the family. In one case the ghost showed similar feelings by turning the lights on and the heat up when the family was expected home. In another, the ghost had protected a restaurant owner from danger on several occasions. Only one family asked me to remove their story from the manuscript because the increase of ghostly incidents had convinced them that their spirit did not want his story told.

I've compiled sixty first-hand accounts of ghosts encountered in private homes, inns, restaurants and shops. Their spirits range from the benevolent who appear once to say goodbye, or to relay a message before going to the other side, to tormented spirits who died tragically and are caught in their struggle to find closure, to poltergeists and vengeful Native American ghosts released by their disrupted graves.

I have told each story and "Supernatural Moment" as closely as possible to the speaker's own words, so that each account will be as sincere and believable as it was told to me. Again I want to thank all the people who trusted me with their stories and a special thanks to their ghosts for letting us know that they are still with us and that death is not an end.

ONE
NEIGHBORHOOD HAUNTS

The Demarest House

Christine Cole Pen & Ink

The Pond in the Meadow Farm

Some things are hard to let go of, particularly when a person feels that he has been unjustly wronged. In fact, such an event can gnaw away at a person's spirit so intensely that he will relive it long after it occurred, sometimes even into the afterlife. In the 1800s such an event happened to Joseph, Jr. and John Minthorne, or Minturn as the family later became known, causing a conflict that continues to reverberate through an upstairs bedroom of the farmhouse where they lived over one hundred and fifty years ago.

Their home, an 1834 Federal-style Colonial still graces Minturn Road between Warwick and Florida and is known today as "The Pond in the Meadow Farm." Dr. Clayton and Patricia de Haan are its fifth owners.

The de Haans moved in with their four children in 1981. Curiously, it was April Fools' Day. Having looked at the house on a whim, they turned the property into their dream — a gentleman's farm. It was close to Dr. de Haan's new position and it offered Patricia several outbuildings to choose from for her painting studio. The two-story house had an elegant simplicity with its center hall and staircase. On the main floor, a parlor extended the length of the house to the right of the staircase, while to the left was a kitchen and dining room. Four bedrooms occupied the second floor.

Just two weeks after they moved in, their twenty-one-year-old daughter Dorian was jolted out of sleep by a tumultuous argument. Two young men in colonial dress raged at one another. One demanded, "This farm is mine!" "The hell it is," the other retorted, "you heard him say he left the house and barns to me. There's no fightin' it." "We'll see about that," the first one sneered as he swung at his opponent. By this time Dorian was sitting bolt upright. She watched the dimly lit scene being played like a movie before her in disbelief. She then sunk ever so slowly under the covers and prayed that she wouldn't be spotted. The room thundered with the bulk of the men's bodies banging into furniture and walls. They rolled over one another into the hallway where they continued to fight.

By now Dorian was certain that everyone in the house was awakened. She listened for her parents' bedroom door to open. Surely her mother would insist that her father investigate the racket. But no doors opened. Could it be that she was the only one who heard what seemed to be a brothers' brawl?

Dorian listened as the voices tumbled down the stairs and into the back meadow. Soon they became so distant they disappeared. She laid dead still until she heard the first person rise the next morning. As each person was up and about she asked, "Were you awakened last night by the sound of men arguing?" Each family member regarded her incredulously. She then told them about the two young men in dark pants, jackets, boots and hats whose rift swirled before her eyes, and then out her bedroom door, downstairs and into the meadow. Her brothers instantly made the most of this rare opportunity to tease her.

Three years later the event was almost forgotten when the de Hanns were invited to a cocktail party at Elaine S. Baird's home. Elaine lived on Denton Lane, which had once belonged to the Minturn Farm's original 120 acres.

Glad to finally have an opportunity to get to know her neighbors, Elaine asked Patricia if she had met the two ghostly brothers who occupied her house yet? Patricia smiled warily and asked, "What do you mean?" Elaine then told the de Haans the history of the Minturn Farm.

When Joseph Minthorne, Sr. became bedridden in 1839, he composed an agreement with his two sons to assure that he and their mother Sarah could live in their home during their remaining years while their sons maintained the farm. According to C.S. Weidman in her article, "Minturn House: Then and Now a Living Trust," the brothers agreed to clean both the barn and the shed and to 'furnish all the firewood at their parents' door.' The main farmhouse, barns and the majority of the 120 acres were given to Joseph, Jr., while John was given the southeast corner of the farm where he had already built a house next to the family burial ground. This area of the farm is where Denton Lane stands today. According to legal records, both brothers signed the document stating that they would uphold their father's request. However, the one hundred-and-fifty-year-old legend is that the Minthorne brothers were not at all happy with the division. At least, John was not.

The brothers are said to have fought bitterly until Joseph's death in 1847. One has only to read the dates on the Minthorne headstones that peak out of the field on Denton Lane to see that Joseph, Jr. and his father died within only two months of each other. Did the brothers' fisticuffs end fatally? However their lives ended, it is apparent that their rift continues through some strange time phantasm.

It has been written that on moonless nights, both brothers still argue in the back bedroom oblivious to modern occupants. Two men in dark clothes — pants, jackets, hats — facing each other at the foot of the bed, gesturing angrily, speaking sharply, always in the back bedroom. Always arguing.

Screams Out on Pine Hill Road

A blood curdling scream, followed by a dreadful moan, awakens the Darling family. It has happened before. It is as daunting as ever, yet Kent and Margarita don't bother to search their house except to check on their four-year-old son, Alexander. They know that the screamer is no longer alive. From tracing their home's history, they even feel certain they've identified the tortured soul. This shrill plea for help has spiraled through their Victorian farmhouse for over one hundred years.

Besides the dreadful screams, Kent and Margarita often hear two women talking in pale murmurs. They check to see if the TV was left on. You know by now that it wasn't. Sometimes the sound of piano playing floats through the halls as soft as a bed sheet falling over furniture. You're probably wondering if they have a piano. They don't.

The Darlings moved into the old Raynor House in 1981. The first disturbance happened as they unpacked their boxes. To stay out of his parents' way, Alexander busied himself by rolling marbles down the second story's slanted hallway into the bathroom. One suddenly hurled out of the bathroom and just missed his head before it ricocheted off the opposite wall. Terrorized, Alexander sank into tears. He learned that afternoon that unseen forces often lurk around corners. Unfortunately, he is uneasy to this day to be alone on the second floor where his bedroom is located.

The Darlings' property was once part of a 400-acre farm owned by William and Susan Wisner Raynor. The original farmhouse burned down and the present home was built in the early 1800s in its place. It is where Gabriel and Fanny Colwell Raynor raised their seven children. None of the children ever married and the house was eventually left to the two surviving daughters, Frances and Martha.

In 1900 one of their farm hands broke into their home because he suspected that they had money stashed in the walls. When the women adamantly denied that there was any money in the house, he attacked and brutally beat them, thinking they would beg for mercy and reveal their hiding spots. Martha died within a few weeks and

Frances died a few months later from the injuries. Martha was forty-nine and Frances was sixty-three. The farm hand was never captured and went unpunished.

A strange woman was recently spotted crossing the lawn. A friend stopped by; finding no one home he turned to leave when he caught sight of her wearing a long, gray dress. He called after her to see if she knew when the Darlings would be back. Without speaking she vanished as she passed the large oak supporting Alexander's tree house. When he relayed this incident later Margarita, who has always had an uncanny penchant for the supernatural, asked, "What did you feel?" "I felt her name was Franny," he answered.

Did the caller intuitively pick up Franny's name from Margarita or does Franny Raynor still roam the very property where she and her sister met such a violent end?

My Father's Calling Card

A few years ago, I received a phone call from a friend of my sister Stacy's, Gail began. Her name was Robin and she was living in the house that had belonged to my family before my parents passed away.

"Gail," she asked, "did anyone ever die in this house?" "Yes, why?" I replied hesitantly. "Well, a couple of funny things are happening," Robin stammered. Suddenly, I knew what she was going to say. It was an occurrence I hadn't thought about since my brothers and sisters and I sold the house.

This account was told to me by a woman who has lived in Warwick most of her adult life. She asked me to change her name along with the others in her story to protect their privacy. Otherwise, this story is told word for word.

"Like what?" I asked, feeling the hair rise on the back of my neck. "Well," Robin said, "there are these rocks that keep being piled in the basement." "You've got to be kidding me," I said, remembering. I had almost succeeded in forgetting about them. I never even told my sisters and brothers about the rock pile. Robin went on to say she and her family had removed the rocks several times, but they always reappeared, so out of exasperation they had decided to leave them where they were. "Also," she continued, "whenever our dog is in the basement he goes to the same corner and barks and paws the wall. Did any of these things ever happen when your family lived here?" she asked tentatively.

"As a matter of fact, they did," I told her. I first noticed the rock pile in the basement shortly after my father died. I saw it a couple of times before I remembered to ask my mother what they were doing there. When asked, Mother replied, "I believe your father has placed them there and would like them to stay, so I've left them." Intrigued that my mother would even consider anything having to do with the paranormal, I pressed for details.

We lived in an Arts and Crafts style bungalow. The house had a recessed porch across the front with bold, tapered columns at either corner overhung by a heavy roof with a large dormer in its center. Deep eaves shaded the house on all sides, which cooled us during the summer. The builder used different textures by siding the main level of the house in wooden clapboards and the second level with shingles that rose up into the roof peaks on either side. The clapboards were painted white and the shingles were green.

My dad always parked his car in the detached garage out back. Then he came in the side door, which entered on a landing between the basement and kitchen.

One afternoon when he came home from work as usual, he stumbled as he started to climb the stairs and tumbled down to the basement. He died as he reached the floor. Later, we found that he had suffered a heart attack.

Soon afterwards, my mother noticed a pile of rocks on the basement floor. They weren't pebbles from the driveway, but the large fieldstones from the farmer's wall that bordered our backyard. Thinking they were the prank of some neighborhood kids, she lugged the rocks outside and dumped them in the woods.

The following day, she came home to the same pile of rocks stacked in the same way. Annoyed, she took the rocks outside and heaved them in different directions. She then locked the garage and house doors, which she had never done before.

She returned to the same pile of rocks arranged in the same way the next day. This went on until eventually my mother came to accept that my father put the rocks there and it was his wish that they remain.

Why Robin's dog was drawn to one corner of the basement still remains a mystery. Perhaps the rock piler himself stood in the corner to make sure his calling card wasn't disturbed. Did the dog sense my father's spirit? We'll never know.

Robin's husband's job relocated and her family moved within a year after her phone call. Now a friend of my other sister lives there. Do I dare ask if the rocks still heap themselves at the bottom of the basement stairs?

The Ghost in the Barn

"In the market for buying a house?" Mildred asked the young couple who walked through her office door.

It was May, 1974. The trees wore their new, fresh green leaves and the air smelled of wet earth and flowers. Andrew and Jan were excited to start their search for an old farmhouse in Warwick, New York.

"Oh, we have plenty of those," Mildred assured them. She had recently re-listed the farmhouse from the former Cedar Cliff Farm out on Jessup Road. It overlooked a meadow of wetlands and the rolling hills of a neighboring dairy farm. It was a modest house with a modest price, perfect for a young couple buying their first home.

Mildred was selling the house for another couple who'd bought it a year earlier. After just seven months, they moved in with friends and placed it back on the market. They claimed it was haunted.

Mildred didn't believe in ghosts and thought they were superstitious or just not used to living in the country. This couple seemed heartier. They were from California. Jan was an elementary school teacher and Andrew was a carpenter. They had a natural, "back to basics" flair about them. They looked forward to growing their own vegetables and keeping a horse. The house needed work, but who better than a carpenter and his family to live there.

"I have just the house to show you," Mildred announced as she turned onto Grand Street and headed out of the village. It's a sixty-three-year-old Colonial on nearly two acres. It once belonged to a twenty-one-acre farm, but like so many of our farms, its owners sold parcel after parcel as taxes rose."

As they rode up the driveway, Jan and Andrew saw the white house through two tangled, lilac bushes. It was a simple vernacular farmhouse that was built into the bank of a hill. It was two-and-a-half stories with a side-gabled roof, a center entrance and an upper and lower porch across the front. To the right of the house was a barn dotted with small hinged windows that were used to ventilate onions.

Mildred could feel the couple's enthusiasm as she led them through the ten rooms. She knew they imagined crackling fires in the fireplace and wood stove, family gatherings on Christmas, and babies in the nursery. Then she gave them time alone to walk the land and explore the barn.

Andrew scanned the inside of the barn for workshop potential, while Jan searched out a corner to build their stable. Deep in thought, they jumped when an elderly man in overalls walked out of the coal bin room. A smile crinkled from his eyes as he said, "Don't let me scare ya, it's just me. I heard you were comin'. My name is Gus Armstrong. I built this house, so let me know if you have any questions." Jan quickly asked, "Why is the ladder to the attic in the bathroom?

Gus drew deeply on his pipe as if getting ready to tell a long story. "When I was first married, my father gave me a twenty-one-acre parcel of his farm as a wedding gift. He owned 150 acres that spanned from Cemetery Road all the way to Taylor. Only they don't call it Cemetery anymore, now it's called Spanktown. Who came up with that one, I'll never know. The name of this road's been changed, too. It used to be called Armstrong after us. But then they changed the town lines and I guess no one saw the point of keeping our name when we didn't own much of the land anymore. By then Pop and his beloved Cedar Cliff Farm were long gone."

"Anyway, the land came with the barn where we used to keep our carriages. Since we didn't use them anymore, I converted it into a house for Mary and me. Mary always wanted a cape, so we kept the hayloft to use as a sleeping quarters for our children. The ladder was placed above the first floor's staircase, because that's where the staircase to the attic would have gone had I gotten around to it. There really wasn't anywhere else to put it. It gets hotter than hell up there in July and August — that's why I put on the sleeping porch. All of us slept out there most of the summer."

"We also had a summer and winter kitchen. People today don't see the point of having two kitchens, so the winter kitchen was made into a bedroom about thirty-years-ago."

"What are the floors and moldings made of?" Andrew asked. "They're fir," Gus said, "Back then that's all I could afford." "How long did you live on Cedar Cliff Farm?" Andrew asked. "All my life," Gus answered righteously, as if there was no other answer.

When Jan and Andrew joined Mildred back in the house they announced they'd take it. Mildred was surprised they decided so quickly, most sales took at least three or four showings. She drove them back to her office to start the paper work. "When did you know this house was for you?" Mildred asked. Jan said, "I thought it was as soon as we pulled into the driveway, but I was certain when Gus told us about the sleeping porch." "Who's Gus?" Mildred laughed. "Gus Armstrong!" the couple responded, "He still takes care of the place."

A look of recognition flashed across Mildred's face as she remembered that the Armstrong family had originally owned the farm. "Where did you see him?" Mildred asked tentatively. "He was in the barn," Jan answered.

Mildred examined the couple before her. "Had the other young couple been right? Was the house really haunted?" she thought. "Mr. Armstrong passed away years ago," she said slowly with a straightforward manner.

She could see by their amazement that they should have more time to decide whether to buy this house. "Why don't you go home and sleep on it for awhile," she suggested. Andrew asked if they could be alone for a moment. As Mildred left to pour herself a cup of coffee in the staff kitchen, she pondered, "Was it possible that Mr. Armstrong appeared in the barn?" More certain seemed the realization that she had just lost a sale.

When she returned to her office, Jan and Andrew smiled. "We've decided to take the house," they chimed, "And Gus can stay as long as he likes," Jan added.

Mr. Hartwick

Jeff and I bought a tiny salt box cottage out on Route 94. It's on the left as you leave Warwick and head toward the village of Florida, Diane Pell began. It was 1978 and our son, Ben was a year-and-a-half. The house was 100 years old, with white washed clapboards and a porch across the front. It was our first house. We bought it from our friend Gay, who owned it for only one or two years. However, the house was better known as the residence of its former owner, Mr. Hartwick.

Diane is a photographer and long-time resident of Warwick. Petite with short, brown hair and an expressive, pixie-like face, she was the first person to answer my ad. Her open, warm manner was so soothing that I felt as if I had known her for years. She actually told me a few stories, but this was the only one that took place in Warwick.

Mr. Hartwick was a sweet, simple old man who occupied himself during the summer months growing berries. He sold his produce at his makeshift stand alongside the highway, where he enjoyed chatting with his customers more than his meager earnings. It wasn't uncommon for him to leave his stand unattended with a coffee can in his place to collect his money. Such country honor systems are still familiar in Warwick. He lived in the house most of his adult life. And it was there that he outlived his wife and remained until his own death and perhaps a bit afterwards.

I felt his presence the first time I stepped onto the porch. I can't explain it really, it was similar to the feeling that someone is looking at you and you turn and they are. I wasn't frightened. I don't think I really believed my instincts in the beginning.

Soon after we settled, Ben and I began hearing strange noises. Sometimes they would sound like a squirrel scratching in a gutter pipe, only we didn't have gutters and the sound came from inside the next room. Ben would look up from playing and ask, "What's that?" There were other noises, bangs and little tapping sounds that seemed attention seeking. For months Ben and I continued to hear these nudgey noises. However my husband never heard anything. When we insisted, he placated us by saying what we heard was probably the field mice that occasionally came in the house.

I always felt that someone was there. I remember doing the dishes with my back to the front door and often feeling compelled to stop, dry my hands and answer the door. It was as though someone was always coming and going. From time to time Ben would tell me, "Mommy, somebody's here." I would open the front door, certain he was right, and feel silly when no one was there.

This went on until one afternoon when I went to see my chiropractor. He cheerfully asked, "How's everything going and how's that new house of yours?" "Everything is wonderful," I heard myself say, "but my house is haunted." I couldn't believe I said that. I never told anyone except my husband, and somehow saying it out loud seemed to validate my suspicions. Until then I had dismissed the occurrences as having some explanation other than the supernatural. Yet, on some level I was sure it was Mr. Hartwick.

The doctor looked at me gravely and said, "As soon as we're done with your adjustment, I want you to tell my wife what you've just told me. She's had a lot of experience with the paranormal and may be able to help you."

His wife, who we'll call Elaine, was an archeologist and anthropologist and was well known for being the first person to open tombs on the Yucatan Peninsula. She invited me into their home, which was attached to the office. She had a sincere, quiet voice that made me feel uneasy, given the sudden seriousness of the situation. I explained that Mr. Hartwick had died peacefully in the house and was found three days later sitting in his armchair. "Well that explains it," Elaine said. "Many times when a person gently passes away, his spirit doesn't know he has died and that's why he remains."

She instructed me on how to help Mr. Hartwick come to terms with his death and leave his earthbound home. "Address him by name and tell him he's passed on and it's time he began his journey. Tell him you live in his house now and that you will be sure to take good care of it."

Spooked Mice

Christine Cole Pen & Ink

28

The next time I felt his presence, I had the long talk that Elaine suggested. I tried to comfort him by saying things like, "I know you're confused," and, "It must be difficult to leave a lifetime behind." I never felt his restive spirit again.

Months later I ran into Gay and told her about my experiences with the ghost of Mr. Hartwick. She sheepishly glanced away and said, "So you felt him, too."

The Resident Trickster at the Demarest House

Looking for the first time at the worn, ghostly, white house with its towering Gothic entryway situated on a small rise in the hamlet of New Milford, Beth suspected a haunting presence. She was standing on the front lawn with her husband, Will, another couple who were their close friends, and the realtor. It was a whiskey-colored fall day and the crisp scent of rotting leaves and apples wafted from the surrounding farms. Mounds of cabernet-colored mums and blood-red sedum waved slightly among the dead husks of lilies that lined the front porch. Beth was listening to the realtor tell them that the house was built in the early 1800s when she and her girlfriend heard a woman crying. The quiet sobs were coming from upstairs, inside the house. Their husbands didn't seem to notice. Already in love with the house and not a person who spooks easily, Beth told Will she believed the house was right for them. "It cries for us," she said.

Shortly after Beth and Will moved in with their two daughters, Erin, age eleven, and Galen, age one month, they noticed their belongings turned up in odd places. It began subtly.

First, Beth found her daughter's picture removed from her desk and placed downstairs in the keeping room. "I wonder if Will wanted this picture where more people will see it," she thought as she went back to her daily activities, soon forgetting the incident. Then she noticed no matter where she put her pewter candlestick, it always appeared on the mantle.

Around that time Beth began to hear a woman singing whenever she was home alone with the baby. "It's hard to explain," she said. "It was this soft, lilting voice that sounded as if I had left a radio on somewhere in the house. You know, when you think you've turned it off, but you didn't quite turn the knob all the way and later you hear music playing ever so softly."

When her daughter, Erin, was home alone she also heard the ghost, but she was hardly serenaded. The ghost taunted her by calling her name over and over in her mother's voice. Exasperated, Erin would yell, "What do you want?!" And then the phantom teasing would stop.

Erin was the only member of the household who saw the ghost. This occurred when she had a girlfriend over to spend the night. The two girls slept in the large, iron bed in one of the guest rooms. During the night, they awoke to see a woman with long dark hair in a white nightgown looking down at them. They screamed and dove under the covers. When they peeked to see if the woman was still there, she was gone.

Another time the ghost appeared to Erin in a different form. Or was it a different ghost? Beth, Will, and Galen went on a short vacation, leaving Erin with her grandmother who lived nearby. Erin forgot one of her schoolbooks and walked home to get it. When she reached the house she realized she had left her key at her grandmother's and began to climb in a first-floor window. A screeching death mask with Native American-like feathers and paint swooped up beside her. Petrified, she lost her balance and fell into the rose bushes. With arms and legs sliced from thorns, she ran to her grandmother's. The gruesome figure hurtled on her heels. Because of this incident, Erin was not willing to talk with me. She didn't want to be reminded of these frightening sightings.

Oddly enough, Beth never found these psychic manifestations threatening. She even recalls them as comforting. "She was the most active around the holidays," Beth recalls. "One year I was home alone with the baby the day before Christmas Eve. I spent the whole day baking, while Galen slept in a baby seat on the kitchen table. All afternoon phantom footsteps could be heard walking up and down the back staircase."

One of the stranger incidents Beth experienced was when Will brought home a Bishon Frise puppy. "Before she was housebroken, we used to tie her in the backyard at night. One evening her barking awakened my husband and me. I went outside to see what was wrong. The dog's collar and chain had been taken off and were lying on the ground beside her. She seemed upset, so I brought her inside and put her in the basement. She was too little to climb the stairs, so I felt certain she'd stay there. When I climbed back in bed Will asked, 'Why did you do that?' 'What?' I answered. 'Why did you put the puppy upstairs?' For a second I wondered if I'd lost my mind. I told him I'd put the puppy in the basement. Hearing her scratches and cries from the third floor, we went to look for her. She was in a bathroom, which was locked from the inside."

Another time, when Galen was a little older, I heard her giggling in the front hall. When I checked on her, she was dancing with her arms outstretched as though she was holding hands with an adult. Sparks sprang from her heels each time one of her shoes hit the parquet floor.

Beth's ghost was an active member of her household for five years and then suddenly vanished. She and her family never knew who the ghost was or why she chose to remain with them during that time. "I miss her," Beth said. "When she was here, I never felt alone." Erin, however, is glad she's gone.

The family interviewed for this story sold their home shortly afterwards to the Elliots. Do we dare ask? The answer is "Yes." Since Linda and Ron Elliot and their daughters, Ashley and Marisa, have moved in, they've noticed several strange happenings. Every once in a while the phantom odor of fish wafts through their 12,000 square foot house. Yes, 12,000 square feet! Marisa is often awakened by the sound of children giggling in the attic. She often considers going upstairs to catch a glimpse of them, but before she is fully awake she is lulled back into a deeper sleep. She has come to look forward to this sound because of the sense of peace it gives her.

According to the New Milford Historical Society's book "New Milford N.Y. — A Historic Tour" the house was built by David Demarest back in 1800. Demarest was an enterprising man who owned and operated six mills. Many of the social affairs of this hamlet revolved around him and his wife and their six children. Could the children heard by Marisa Elliot be a swish of psychic energy that flows through the house like a timeless river?

The Ghosts of Wawayanda Creek Farm

So many things happened during the four years we lived in the farmhouse at Wawayanda Creek that I could go on forever. I can't tell you where the house is. If people were to find out, the house would be dubbed with the sobriquet "Haunted House" and the present owners would be inundated with caravans of gawkers driving by at all hours.

The house was built during the 1700s where Long House Indians once settled. Our boys often found arrowheads and once I uncovered a small grinding stone. A former owner found a piece of Native American pottery that is now in The Museum of Natural History.

I never liked the house, but for my husband, Leo, it was a dream come true. It was a lumbering, three story Colonial that had been added onto during the 1850s and again at the turn of the century. It had layers of walls and floors that we soon learned each exuded its own ghostly remnant of history.

We bought the farm in 1969. It was badly in need of repair, so we rented part of it out and came up from Long Island on weekends to work on the vacant wings. We didn't actually move in year round with our five children until May of 1971.

The house stood like a sentinel on one of Warwick's most bucolic back roads. It had a wrap-around porch and grand double oak doors that led into the front hall. The parlors on either side had painted mantles and amber, pine plank flooring. I don't know why I did this, but the first time I entered the house I turned to the realtor and asked, "Is this house haunted?" "Not that I know of," she replied and quickly changed the subject.

The first disturbance occurred when I tried to close the paneled pocket doors that led from the east parlor into the dining room. The dining room was drafty and I wanted to warm it by shutting the doors and lighting a fire in the fireplace. One door slid easily to the center of the doorway, but the other wouldn't budge. I tugged and tugged to release it. It seemed to be painted in place. When I stopped to think of another plan, the door suddenly shot across the doorway and slammed into its mate. Crack! I nearly rocketed up to the ceiling. Later, I tried to convince myself that maybe I snapped a spring or something with all my pulling and jiggling. However I never trusted those doors again.

After that, whenever I walked into the dining room, I sensed someone behind me. Often, I felt a light tap on my shoulder. Of course, when I turned around no one was there. I still get chills just thinking about it.

The dining room had a back staircase that led up to three bedrooms. This was the oldest part of the house and it didn't connect to the rest of the rooms on the second floor. Perhaps it was once used as a sleeping quarters for servants. My two older sons, Mark and Matthew, chose this area for their bedrooms because it was isolated and they felt as though they had their own apartment.

One of the bedrooms had old, water stained, floral wallpaper and always felt cold. The boys thought the room was creepy, so we stuck our old pull out couch in there and used it as a guest room.

Our first guest was a friend of mine. After sleeping in the room one night, she demanded to spend the next night in a different room. When I asked why, she shuddered, "I can't talk about it yet."

Years later, she would tell me that a violent shaking of the bed awakened her and a sudden iciness filled the room. Then the heavy pull-out bed levitated three feet into the air and abruptly slammed to the floor. She immediately stumbled downstairs and lay awake on a couch in one of the parlors for the rest of the night.

Since at the time I didn't know why she refused to sleep in that room, I continued to put guests there. Mark had a friend stay over who became frightened also. He said while he was lying in bed a beam of light appeared, morphed into a giant ball and floated around the room. When the room finally became dark again, he was kept awake by rustling noises he couldn't identify. He spent the night often, but wouldn't sleep in that room again until a year and a half later when the same mysterious beam of light appeared, accompanied by the dreadful sound of a man moaning.

I sought answers from a friend who claimed to be psychic. She said she felt an angry presence in the guest room. She suggested I get rid of the old wallpaper and paint the room a cheery color to give it a more positive energy. Eager to take action, I painted the room yellow and bought bright curtains and a throw rug and turned it into a TV room. The look was that of a cozy family room, but the damp chill persisted. One night I was watching TV with my daughter, Kate, when a candlestick flew off the top of the TV and just missed our feet.

Another time when both my daughters had friends over for the night, they each heard knocking on the walls and moaning noises and thought it was the other sister and her friend trying to scare them. When they simultaneously arrived in my room to tell on one another, we realized the sound was coming from the TV room. My husband was on a camping trip with the boys, so I was left on my own to reassure them. I felt I had to prove that no one was there, but I was too frightened to go and look. I called up the back staircase. A dim glow came from the TV room and then faded. I called again and it recurred. That night the girls camped out in my bedroom, so we could all be together. We slept with the lights on. I wondered why my happy children and their bustle of activity didn't squelch these unseen forces.

My two older sons had an experience while the rest of us were away. We were visiting my mother in Massachusetts and the boys wanted to stay home. Mark was a senior in high school and Matthew a junior. Of course, they had their friends over and were having a great time when a man knocked on the door to ask for directions. The boys invited him in and decided to scare him by telling him we had a ghost.

The man said he knew how to get rid of ghosts and promptly yelled obscenities and demanded that the ghost leave. Stunned and frightened that a line of respect had been crossed, the boys coaxed the man to leave. As he drove his van down the street, his brakes slammed to the floor by themselves and sent him into the windshield. He drove back with a bloody nose and mouth and nastily demanded to know what was going on. The boys cringed behind the locked door and phoned the police. Mark still wonders if the van driver, himself, was a ghost trying to scare them. Once you live in a haunted house, you learn that anything is possible.

Many of the disturbances took place while one of us was napping. One afternoon, when Matthew was home alone, he put the dog outside and went upstairs to lie down. Later, he was awakened by the dog licking his hand. When Matt passed through the kitchen to let the dog out again, he saw two young girls in old-fashioned dresses sitting on the radiator giggling. When he told me this, I asked, "What did you do?" "I went back to bed and hoped they'd go away," he shrugged. I think we all tried to deal with the spirits who lived with us in that way. From time to time, we each saw a man in dark clothing walk down the main staircase. We each knew he was not of this world and felt that our home belonged more to its past than it did to us.

Another time, I was jolted from a nap by a crushing sensation as if someone heavy thudded on top of me. After a few seconds of struggling, I realized no one was there. That was too much. I told my husband that I was sick of sharing our home with hostile dead people. They would have to reenact the trapped remnants of their lives without me. I wanted to move. The incidents were so disjointed I never knew what to expect. I was exhausted.

The whole family agreed. My husband thought he was going to enjoy the history and charm of our old house, but instead, he, too, was worn down by its imposing presence.

Shortly after that, we hung a "For Sale" sign in the front yard. When a couple of antique dealers from New York were seriously interested in buying it, I felt obliged to tell them that the house was haunted. They were thrilled. "It's only fitting that a 200-year-old Colonial in the country has ghosts," they assured us.

A couple of years later, a mutual friend of ours told me the antique dealers spot a Native American specter once in a while. They are said to have had a cocktail party one Christmas, where several wine glasses careened across the room scattering their guests and bits of crystal.

Sometimes I think of visiting them to compare stories, but then I decide some things are better left unsaid.

Robert

It began as just noises. About a year after we moved in, I began to hear someone walking up and down the stairs or rattling around in the kitchen. For a while, my husband, Jeff, and I thought it was our cat. After months of hearing this sound, I asked Jeff if he thought we had a ghost. He told me I was nuts, until one night when he and his buddy had a ghostly experience of their own. They were watching TV in the loft over our living room when a heavy, glass ashtray clattered across the tabletop on its own volition.

Laura Duncan, a tall striking blond settled in a chair at our dimly lit table in the tavern where she worked. It was the end of her evening bartending shift and she lit a cigarette to relax. She spoke in a wonderful, deep, throaty voice that would make even Lauren Bacall envious. At the time of this interview, she lived with her husband, Jeff, and their three boys in Greenwood Lake. Built in 1938, their house was originally a summer bungalow with a fieldstone fireplace and lots of knotty paneling. Although the house had been updated and added onto, it still retained much of its Adirondack cabin feel.

After that, the incidents came closer together, or maybe we noticed them more because we both acknowledged them. We listened to the nightly ritual of ghostly footsteps treading from room to room. He would creak down the hallway of the first floor and go into my youngest son's bedroom. Then we'd hear him climb the stairs, step! step! step! And closer ... step! step! Closer. Then the footfalls would pass our bedroom and walk down the hall toward our two other sons' bedrooms. After that, they always stopped. It seemed as though he was checking on us.

Another time, I'm certain the ghost helped me find my son's ear medicine dropper. My middle son was ill and I was in a panic. It was time to give him his medicine and I couldn't find the dropper. I hunted frantically, pulling everything apart. I went into the kitchen one last time and there was the dropper in the middle of the counter where I couldn't miss it. I'm positive it wasn't there before.

From then on, I thought our ghost was someone who watched out for us. I became even more convinced one summer while Jeff was away on a catering job in Maryland. During that time I felt comforted each evening as I heard the ghost make his nightly rounds. One night I was lying in bed reading when I heard footfalls walk past my bedroom door. When I glanced up, I saw a tall man wearing a camelhair jacket. It was so vivid I was certain he was an intruder. Scared to death, I tiptoed through the whole house checking every room. No one was there and all the doors and windows were locked. Realizing I had just seen our home's guardian, I slid back into bed and was able to pick up my book where I left off. I was intrigued and amazed, but not frightened.

Another time we had a group of friends over for the evening. They loved to hear our haunted house tales and asked me to dig out my Ouija Board. We asked our ghost to tell us his name. We were hardly touching the pointer when it spelled out the name R-O-B-E-R-T quite deliberately.

Occasionally, out of the corner of my eye, I see a tall figure drift past. Last fall I saw him as clearly as I see you at this moment. For three consecutive nights I was awakened by a tapping sound at the foot of our bed. It would become more insistent as it worked its way toward my head. On the third night I must have dangled my arm off the side of the bed in my sleep, because I was jolted awake when someone smacked it hard with the palm of his hand. I spun around and caught Robert standing over me. He vanished immediately.

Recently he did something even more startling. He tapped me on the back while I was napping on the couch in our living room. Thinking it was one of the boys, I turned to see who it was. No one was there. Determined to continue my nap, I repositioned myself and again, shut my eyes. This time something deliberately jabbed me and shouted, "Laura!" in a gravelly man's voice. I was flabbergasted. I didn't know ghosts could talk.

Robert doesn't like being overlooked and makes his presence known the most during the holidays and especially when my parents are visiting. He seems to enjoy turning the heat to tropical heights and the dishwasher on at all hours of the night whenever they are our guests.

For whatever reason, Robert is here to stay. We've come to accept him as part of our household and feel safer knowing he watches over us.

Button, Button, Who Sewed the Button?

Pat Moore Lesando was born and raised in the hamlet of Sugar Loaf. In 1971, she and her first husband Vinnie rented a green, asphalt-shingled cottage on Pine Hill Road from her cousins. The house had been in Pat's family for generations. When this mysterious incident took place, she had recently given birth to their daughter, Jody-Lynn, and was a homemaker while Vinnie worked the graveyard shift at Chester Cable.

Shortly after the Lesandos moved in, Vinnie came home from work one morning, as usual, and mentioned that the button from his pants had fallen off the night before. Pat asked if he still had the button. When he replied yes, she said, "Leave it in your pocket and I'll sew it on before you go back to work tonight." Pat took out her green thread and placed it on the table as a reminder. The day flew by with the needs of her newborn and she forgot to repair her husband's pants.

Later that evening when Vinnie dressed for work, he said, "Thanks for sewing my button. I know how busy you were today." Pat was dumbfounded. "I didn't sew your button. That must be a different pair of pants." Vinnie replied, "No they aren't. I took these off the back of the kitchen chair where I left them this morning." Pat asked him to check his pocket for the button. He pulled out a button identical to its replacement. A spectral button had been sewn above his fly with the very thread that still sat on the table. Thinking that she was losing her mind, Pat fell apart.

Vinnie stayed home that night to console her, but he couldn't explain away the strange event. Knowing how much Pat adored her grandmother, Emily Holbert, he pleaded with Pat to try to get some sleep and suggested that she invite her grandmother over the following day.

Pat took his advice and invited her for lunch. Emily Holbert was known to her family and friends as a clairvoyant. She had an Old World way about her, which prompted her family to refer to her as a gypsy. Pat confided what had happened the day before. Emily listened and said, matter-of-factly, "It must have been your Aunt Ivy who sewed the button."

Aunt Ivy had been married to Emily's brother. She and her husband had also rented the green cottage when they were first married. Tragically, Aunt Ivy became ill and passed away a few short years later. From then on, Emily raised Ivy and her brother's children.

"She must have seen how busy you were and stepped in to help out," Emily surmised.

The Ghost in the Attic

May blessings be about you; beautiful vale of Warwick; may your fields and forests be as green, your waters as bright, the cattle on your hundred hills as fruitful as in the days of old.
Frank Forester 1807-1858

We rented the Hubbard House out on Ackerman Road for four years. It was a rambling, two hundred-year-old Colonial with a porch across the front that was trellised on either side with tangled vines. The property was once a grand estate. It echoed of wealth and splendor through its outbuildings that included an icehouse and a gardener's cottage. The yard had an ancient feel with its bramble covered tennis courts, crumbling swimming pool, and terraced waterfalls. Built around 1780, it was reminiscent of romance and harbored a heartsick specter who held onto her pain like a timeless oil lamp.

Shortly after Annie Colonna and Russell Chere were married they moved to Warwick from New York City. It was April of 1991. Annie is a potter and sculptress who teaches art to children in the village of Warwick. She is tall and thin with short, dark hair that glistens auburn in the afternoon sun. Her flair for style is apparent in the way she dresses. On the summer afternoon I invited her to my home to tell her story, she wore a black shirt of casual, natural fabric with pants that seemed to wrap their exotic sienna print around her long legs. She spoke thoughtfully, in a way that left no doubt of her sincerity.

The Spider

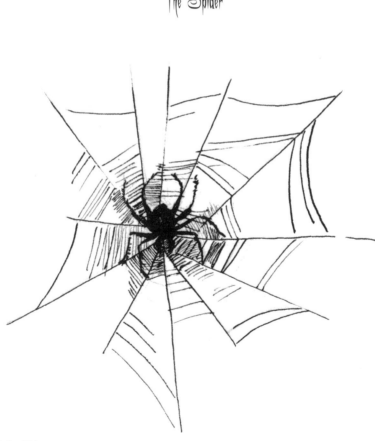

Christine Cole Pen & Ink

Annie began by describing the house. Downstairs there was a large L-shaped living room and dining area with wide, pine plank flooring. In some places the boards were so worn we could see into the cellar. The kitchen was old and dingy with a huge brick fireplace that was once used for cooking. The area in front of it was probably considered the "keeping room" during the colder months. At the rear of the house, French doors led to what was left of the tennis courts and swimming pool.

During Prohibition, the house had been used as a get-away for a wealthy family who was remembered for their extravagant parties. Among their noted guests were many artists and writers. Sixty years before Prohibition, the house was thought to have been owned or frequented by Warwick's famous sporting writer, Frank Forester.

The walls separating three small bedrooms on the second floor had been torn down to make one expansive, master bedroom. When we lived there, the hall outside our bedroom led to two more bedrooms and bathrooms. Russell used one for an office and I used the other for my studio. At the end of the upper hallway, facing our bedroom was an odd little staircase without a banister. It led to the attic. It wound past a small window that looked out over the front porch roof and across the drive to the icehouse.

The first time I climbed these stairs I felt strangely chilled, even though it was summer and the attic was oppressively hot. Then I felt a change in air density as though someone whisked up behind me and touched the back of my neck with her or his invisible fingers. I panicked and fled to find Russell, who was down in the kitchen. I blurted what I had just felt. He laughed and pointed out how I wasn't frightened when I lived by myself in Brooklyn or New York City, why was I getting the willies in Warwick? I agreed, but didn't brave the attic again for months afterward. It was a large house with lots of storage space, so I really didn't need to go up there.

By the following winter we had accumulated more things and I attempted to explore the attic again to hunt for a spot to keep holiday decorations and boxes of clothing from alternate seasons. Once again, I pressed through a cold spot near the little window, but I convinced myself to shrug it off as a draft. This time, when I opened the door, I was overwhelmed by a strong scent of floral cologne. The scent intensified as I crept into the space. Then the rustling of a stiff petticoat and dress flocked toward me and an invisible body slammed into me so insistently that it almost knocked me over. I dropped the box of clothing and ran. Again I sought Russell and spouted that there was something in the attic that didn't want me there. He knew by my fright to take me seriously and went to investigate. He came back pale and shaken. He gasped that as soon as he stepped through the attic door a shock of panic circuited through his bones like an electrical current. He also bolted down the attic stairs afraid to look behind him. Once he caught his breath, he became cross and snapped, "Don't ever go up there again!" I thought this incident had converted him into a believer. However, the couple of times I brought it up, he insisted that it was my fear that had spooked him and nothing else.

A couple of weeks later, I searched our closets for my favorite winter coat and remembered that it was in the box flung across the attic floor like a hot potato. I dreaded the thought of going to retrieve it. Opening the door hesitantly, I kept one foot on the top step. I scanned the room from corner to corner. It seemed devoid of otherworldly beings, so I hurried inside to whisk out the box. Again, I smelled the pervasive, floral odor. I couldn't identify it, except that it was sickeningly sweet and strong. This time its wearer let me do what I needed, but I was certain she watched me. I could feel her.

44

What was it that bound this woman's spirit to the attic and did it involve the chill always felt near the small window on the staircase, I wondered? An answer reverberated through my head with a strange persistence, almost as if someone had placed it there: a young boy had fallen out of that window and his mother had either also fallen while trying to save him or eventually jumped to her death, overcome with grief.

One evening Russell and I were talking to Tom Woglom who was the caretaker of the property. Tom and his family had lived in the Hubbard House before us. I asked if he ever encountered anything strange while he lived here. "Yes," he laughed. He went on to tell us that when he and his wife, Sally, moved in, Sally was about to give birth to their second child. Their daughter, Abby, was staying with his mother for a few days until the baby arrived home. Sally went into labor in the middle of the night during a bad snowstorm. Tom rushed her to St. Anthony Hospital, where he also spent the night to avoid driving back and forth in foul weather.

The following morning their neighbors who rented the converted icehouse came with flowers and gifts to celebrate the birth of their son. Puzzled, Tom asked, "How did you find out, we've only told my mother and Abby?" "We read your sign, 'It's a boy! His name is David' in the window above your front door." Tom and Sally looked at one another incredulously. "I didn't hang a sign. I haven't even been home yet," Tom insisted. Could his mother have gone into the house this morning and hung the sign, he wondered. No, she didn't have a key and besides she would never drive while it was snowing. Later that morning Tom went home to pick up a few things. When he looked above the door, the window stood empty as always.

Tom's strange story haunted Annie. She continued to be nagged by the suspicion that a woman who had once lived in the house had lost her son when he fell out of the little window on the attic stairs. The thought was as overpowering as the next string of events.

One night when Russell was away on a business trip, I sculpted till around two in the morning. Later when I went to bed, the recurrent floral attar, that until this moment was only noticeable in the attic, wafted over my face. It seemed to descend on me from the window. I thought I was suffocating. Panicked, I frantically hunted for the light switch, while knocking the night-table lamp to the floor. I bolted upright gasping for air and wondering if I had fallen asleep and had a bad dream.

This wraith-like attack occurred three or four more times while we lived there. I'd wake up thrashing for breath certain I was being smothered. The last time this happened I opened my eyes and saw a young woman with light blond hair severely piled on top of her head holding a pillow above my face. I couldn't take my eyes off of her. She wore a long, calico dress with a tight bodice and high, lace collar. As she slowly dissolved before me, I could see that she looked intensely sad. I shook with terror for the rest of the night certain she was going to kill me.

That was the last time I ever saw her tormented spirit or even smelled her perfume. I've lived in several places since, but I still think of her and wonder if her visitations were the result of the tragic loss of her son. Recently, I met a woman who lived in the house with her family twenty-five years earlier. She also underwent an eerie event. She told me she pulled in the driveway from grocery shopping one afternoon and saw her youngest son, Jonathan, hanging upside down out of the little window on the attic stairs. She rushed in the house and demanded to know which of her four other children had dangled their little brother out the window by his ankles. All four stared at her dumbly. None confessed. Jonathan hysterically gasped and coughed, "The lady! The lady!" After that, she forbade them to play on the attic stairs or in the attic.

Was it a woman's grief over the loss of her child that imprisoned her spirit in an attic for all of eternity? Or was it the overwhelming guilt over the fact that she, herself, took her child's life and the resentment she feels over others who continue to find happiness in what was once her home?

The Visit

This story was told to me by Phylis Richards. From 1985 to 2000, Phylis and husband Carl lived on Newport Bridge Road in their custom built home, "The New Old Amity House." Her story is not the typical, mischievous ghost story in which televisions dramatically turn on in the night and doors open by themselves, but a story of a live conversation with someone from the other side.

Carl phoned Phylis to let her know he wanted to stay at his mother's home in New Jersey that evening to begin to put her things in order. His mother had passed away the night before. She had been sick for a long time and a rift was brewing between him and his brother over how her estate should be handled. Phylis hung up the phone, checked on their daughters Amy and Jessica, and got ready for bed.

She and Carl had designed their home to have the conveniences of a new home and the charms of an old. Built in 1985, their house is a warm familial blend of a log cabin and a center-hall Cape Cod. One of the unique characteristics of this house is that every door is an antique from a family member's home. The house is a clapboard and peg journey into the Richards' family heritage.

When Phylis settled into bed, she heard the Victorian, double oak doors creak open and slam shut as someone entered the front hall. "Carl, is that you?" she called.

"No, it's me, Mom," her mother-in-law replied. "Phylis, everything is going to be all right."

This message was typical of the late Mrs. Richards. She was a no-nonsense person who would only come back to say what she needed and then vanish. Phylis never heard her mother-in-law's exit. Instinctively, she knew that she had been comforted with the otherworldly knowledge that Carl and his brother would work out their differences. That night she fell asleep cherishing the privilege of having known her mother-in-law, and the gift she had been given. Phylis now knew what she had always believed, that there is an afterlife.

The next morning Jessica and Amy came down for breakfast. Amy asked, "Where's Daddy?" "He stayed at Grandma's house," Phylis replied. "But I heard him come in," Amy insisted. "I heard that too," Phylis smiled knowingly.

Sisters Reunited

Barbara Riley woke up one morning in her St. Louis home of 16 years and announced, "I'm in the wrong place." It was a realization that instantly made sense. She had been divorced for several years, her parents were getting older and needed her closer, and her children, Shaughn and Alyson, had moved away and begun their own lives. It was time to begin the next chapter of her own. But it was more than that. She felt lured by some outside force, a magnetism, as though something pulled at her heart. She quit her job teaching high school science, sold her home, loaded her belongings into her truck, and drove east.

Her internal compass led her to the Warwick Valley. Its bucolic, rolling hills lay halfway between her mother's home in Bergen County, New Jersey and her father's in Sullivan County, New York. Here, she began her search for "the right place." But like a watched pot that never boils, the right place cannot necessarily be found through a realtor. Day after day was spent searching and nothing seemed quite right. Instead, she stumbled across her home one afternoon while yard sale hunting on the outskirts of the village of Florida.

She knew as she made the turn onto Clarke Road and drove up the winding rise through farm fields that she was headed home. When she saw the 1784 shaker cottage nestled into the hill, tingles shot through her body. The sensation was so overwhelming she nearly passed out. There was no doubt about it; this was the right place, her right place. Forgetting to look at the things for sale, Barbara sought out the house's owner, Pat Fasanella. "This is my house," she said excitedly, before even seeing the inside. "Excuse me?" replied Pat, befuddled. "This is my house. I'm certain of it. I have to live here." "It's not for sale," Pat replied, while stepping back hoping for a polite escape from this crazy woman. "Will you sell it to me?" Barbara tried to reason. "No," she laughed, "we love our house and don't intend to ever leave." "Would you please show me the inside?" Barbara begged.

Once through the front door the tiny house unfolded in front of her exactly as she knew it would. There was a small entry hall with a worn pine tread staircase that led to the second floor. To the right was a quaint living room with a low ceiling. One wall had a large brick, open-hearth fireplace with a wrought iron arm for swinging pots over the fire. To the left of the fireplace stood hand-hewn pine cabinetry where salted meats and kitchen items were once stored. A separate kitchen was added off the back of the house in 1842. Upstairs were two bedrooms and a grandma's attic with slanted ceilings. Pat told her the house was originally a tenant house built on the Poppino Farm. The main house stood on the other side of Clarke Road until it burned down in the 1960s. After the tour, Barbara was completely smitten with the 210-year-old home. She wished she didn't have to leave. "Please remember me if you change your mind. You can reach me by going to any antique store in the village and asking for 'Barbara with the hair.'"

Pat didn't forget the tall woman with the extraordinary, long, thick, wavy, dark hair. Three years later the Fasanella family had to move because of a job relocation. As instructed, Pat drove into the village to the Randallville Mill Antique Shop and asked how she could reach "Barbara with the hair." Owner Gary Randall knew exactly who she meant and called immediately.

Barbara was visiting a friend in Missouri for a long weekend. Before she had time to call and say, "I'll take it," another couple was interested in buying the Early American home. However, this time Pat was relieved to hear from the strange woman with the incredible hair. She confided that the other couple spoke of knocking down walls and building additions. She knew that Barbara would keep the house as it was and love it as she had. Within a month, Barbara owned "the right place."

As soon as it was vacant, she drove up to the house to wallpaper the living room. Her footsteps echoed across the wide plank floors. She couldn't believe it was really hers. Realizing how stuffy the house felt, she tried to open the windows, but they were painted shut. Undeterred she turned on her radio, climbed the ladder and unrolled her first sheet of wallpaper. Suddenly the radio flickered off and on — off and on. Then an icy chill swooped up around her. Barbara knew she had a visitor from the other side. She climbed down the ladder and sat on the floor to comfort the restive entity. As she spoke she divined that the spirit belonged to a twelve-year-old girl who died from having fallen down a well. Her name was Catherine.

Later that month, Barbara was once again led by an invisible hand. This time it was to walk through the farmer's fields that lay in front of her home. The same tingling sensation returned as she neared an open well in the lower field. It was surrounded with overgrown brambles, so the farmer wouldn't drive his tractor into it. Until that moment she had assumed Catherine had fallen into the covered well in back of her home. Now she was certain that it was this well that took her life. Oddly, she had just completed a whimsical garden in the front of her house which she named "The Children's Garden." In it she used a child's iron bed and doll seated in a small chair as ornaments. The doll sat facing the very spot where the well stood in the field below. Did she subliminally build this garden for Catherine? Excited to have pieced together another clue, and saddened by a feeling of loss, Barbara began to feel even more connected to Catherine.

She has invited several psychics into her home hoping to uncover more about Catherine's life. Without being filled in, they all have discerned the same presence, "I feel the spirit of a young girl in this house." One even visualized her body waked in front of the hearth. When I asked Barbara why she thought this ghost beguiled her to move across the country, she, a believer in past lives, responded, "She didn't finish having me as a sister."

From time to time, Catherine's light, quick footfalls still descend the stairs while Barbara is reading in the living room, as though she climbed out of bed to have a late night talk. And once in a while, Barbara feels her sisterly stroke down the length of her hair and has even felt her climb onto her lap. However, it is less and less frequent. Perhaps Catherine needed Barbara to help her resolve her untimely death and is now content to take her place on the other side.

The Triplets' House of Agony

I stepped onto the front porch from the August shade of South Street's tree-lined sidewalk. The house was Victorian with Second Empire styling characterized by its mansard roof and dormer windows that dated it mid-to-late Nineteenth Century. I had been invited by the "triplets," as they were known — long time residents of this old section of Warwick.

I wound the ancient, brass doorbell and listened to its metallic clanging that sounded like the bells we had on our bicycles as children. Seconds later, Bill, Bob, and Henry Aldinger bubbled, "Come in, come in." As I stepped through the worn double doors into the dim entrance hall, I immediately noticed their doorstop. It was a gravestone. Observing my stare, Bob told me it was left by a former owner, it came with the house when they bought it twenty years earlier. He added, "It's part of the charm of the place."

They led me into their dining room. It took a few minutes for my eyes to adjust in the somber light. Despite the summer heat, not a window was open, not a breath of air stirred. The brothers didn't seem to notice. Their furnishings were dark and there was something about the shirred, roman shades on all of the eight-foot-high windows that I found unsettling. It wasn't because they were drawn closed or yellowed from age, or even that they were too feminine for three seventy-year-old bachelors. Then it came to me. They looked like the scalloped satin used to line coffins.

A small oil lamp was placed in the center of the dining room table. The brothers eagerly took their seats and leaned expectantly toward me. Bob giggled, "So you're the lady who's come to exorcise our home." That's when I explained that I wasn't a ghost detective or buster; I was a writer who wanted to write their story for a collection of Warwick ghost tales. I speculated whether the séance-like atmosphere was intentional.

"It all started the day we closed on the house," Bob began. "After we signed the checks I jokingly asked former owner Paula Dickson if we had just bought any unwanted tenants. She hesitated, then confessed, 'There are various happenings, but don't worry, they won't hurt you.'"

The brothers continued their story in relay fashion, one continuing what another began to say. Bill chimed in, "That's when I asked, 'What kind of happenings?'"

The three men twinkled at one another while they savored the answer. It was Henry's turn to finish. "Mrs. Dickson told us that from time to time we'd be visited by a woman in a long, brown dress with high button shoes. She can be seen drifting down the staircase. And occasionally our belongings may hurl across the room."

"Boy, was she right!" Bob added, laughing. "It gets pretty rough here sometimes," Bill nodded. "You can say that again," Henry agreed.

The triplets were hardly put off by Mrs. Dickson's late disclosure. They were used to stories about the other side because their grandfather had been an undertaker. He had taken delight in exposing them as boys to some of the details of his trade that children shouldn't know. These ghoulish tidbits still delighted them, and they chose to relay some of the early mechanics of embalming to me. My head spun in the sweltering closeness. Just as I was about to beg for air,

Bob cracked me up by relaying his grandfather's favorite truism. He had told them from a young age, "The dead will never hurt you, it's those bastards on two feet you need to watch out for."

"Tell me the first supernatural disturbance that occurred after you moved in," I coaxed. "A month after we settled in," Henry blurted, "we were eating dinner when the copper blowtorch we kept on top of our kitchen cabinets rose up and zoomed across the room on its own volition. It smashed onto the floor so hard that it dented." "We have it right here," Bob chimed. "Pick it up. See how heavy it is?" "Look at that dent," Bill added, "that's what happened when it hit the floor!" "Ain't that somethin'?" Bob said still amazed.

I asked if they ever witnessed the female apparition that Mrs. Dickson had warned of. "No," they shook their heads, "but our neighbor Ginny Wrenchen's children did."

Ginny was an ex-Broadway singer and dancer whose ginger-colored hair and swish of importance resembled Beverly Sills. She and her husband had owned the triplets' house before Paula Dickson. "This house had a number of entities locked inside," she whispered. That's when she mentioned that her children often saw a woman on the stairs or in the upper hallway. "Ghosts are most often seen on staircases because that's one of the places where people expend the most energy while they are alive," she said with a tone of expertise. She went on to tell of her and her husband's experiences.

One hot summer afternoon, her husband was reading the paper in his armchair by the fireplace when he felt someone join him in the living room. He looked up expecting to see Ginny or one of their children, but was instead jolted out of his seat by the sight of a hovering, headless man cloaked in black. Ginny confessed she didn't believe him, until she saw the same apparition the following day. It terrified her so badly, she nearly peed her pants. She also admitted that during their years there, they were steadily barraged by objects that flew off their shelves.

Ginny was the former owner who contributed the tombstone. She also installed the shelf of hand-carved marble in the front hall. The brothers enjoy this piece as much as the tombstone and compare it to the Demilunes in funeral parlors where visitors add their names to the condolence book. These are just a couple of the props that set the scene as they revel in their home's macabre history.

After the Wrenchens moved away from South Street, the new neighbors soon suspected that the triplets lived in a vortex of supernatural activity. Of course, they too, befriended the charming brothers who upon their first introduction were irresistible. One afternoon one of the new neighbors dropped by to show them their blueprints for a renovation project. Bill commented, "Well, I don't think this is the best plan, because you don't have any windows on the south side of the house." The neighbor responded, "We did that on purpose." "Why?" all three asked. "Because when we look over at your house in the evenings, we see several men with 1800-style collars staring back at us from your library window." The triplets convinced them not to forgo windows because of their strange inhabitants, but rather to keep shades drawn in the evening on that side of the house.

Next, I was shown into the kitchen to survey where the blowtorch ruckus took place and to regard their unruly dishwasher. The dated, avocado-colored machine sat mutely under the counter with half a roll of duct tape wrapped around its on/off lever. "We had to do that," Bill pointed out, "the bloomin' thing used to switch on by itself at all hours."

"Even after we disconnected it," Bob followed, "then we got smart and taped the lever in the off position. This seemed to work. Ain't that somethin'? It's the same with the lights. We've taped many of their switches off, so they don't run up our electric bill," he explained. "We even installed a peephole in our basement door so we can check if our basement light is on or off."

I treaded downstairs after my hosts, so they could display the small circular glass installed in the door to their workshop. Inside, a workbench and organized shelves lined with baby food jars of nuts, bolts, and nails appeared as though they hadn't been touched in years. At least, not by human hands. Often things are discovered out of place as though unseen forces had been working on a project of their own.

They used the next room as a family room. "This is where the original kitchen was," Bob pointed out. "And it was here that the bodies of the people who died in this house were laid on planks and bled by the undertaker." Again the triplets described some of the intimate secrets of embalming and again I became woozy. I started to think of ways to politely cut the interview short. My legs went rubbery and their voices sounded like they were at the opposite end of a long dark tunnel. "We've learned of eight people who were waked in our living room," Henry added.

"May I have a glass of water?" I interrupted.

I followed them back upstairs and wondered how three elderly men who walked with canes could climb stairs so spryly. When I sat down to drink my water I felt the blood rush back into my head. "Are you all right?" Bill asked. "I'm fine," I lied. "How did you find out that eight people were waked here?" I asked, changing the subject. "Well that's another story," Bill beamed.

"One day a woman named Dorothy Baird Talcott knocked on our door. She had lived in this house for nineteen years and asked if she could revisit. We learned most of the house's history from her and it was she who told us of the eight wakes." Our tour continued to the second floor.

"When we brought Dorothy here to the library she shivered, saying, 'I can't go in there. This was my grandmother's bedroom.'"

One of Dorothy's strongest memories of her grandmother was the sound of her agonizing moans. Another was the horrid smell of death that permeated her bedroom long after she died of cancer. Her mother tried to cover the smell with a steady abundance of fresh-cut flowers. Even worse were Dorothy's memories of the undertaker who came to prepare her grandmother's body: she was asked to assist him by emptying the buckets of her grandmother's blood in the outhouse; then, toss sand in afterwards, so it wouldn't attract flies.

Bob added, "Can you imagine a child being asked to do that? That's somethin', ain't it?"

After hearing these stories the brothers dubbed the library, 'The Room of Agony.' Every once in a while the scent of flowers still wafts throughout the room. Bill described this phantom scent by saying, "Sometimes it smells like a funeral parlor in here."

Most of the disturbances at the Aldinger triplets'residence occur in 'The Room of Agony.' And yet, I viewed this room as an endearing testament to the inseparable existence of these three brothers, particularly its photo gallery — here, three babies dressed identically, there — in Air Force uniforms, there again as tourists in some of the seventy-four countries they visited. Bob told me how when they enlisted in the Air Force in 1943, they asked to be assigned together. They received written permission from the Secretary of War to fly in the same squadron, but never on the same plane. All three evacuated the wounded from the Battle of the Bulge. Touched by the innocent and invincible faces of these photos, I remarked on how handsome they were. Bob sighed modestly, "Oh well, now you see what the ravages of time can do." Born just five minutes apart, they passed through youth and middle age, never married, worked the same jobs, and were now retired together. They've even been known to have the same dreams on the same nights!

Then, out of nowhere, Bill giggled, "You're not going to believe this, but we have a body here right now." Instantly the brothers became lighthearted again. "That's right," Bob gushed, "we have our dear friend Shepard Coleman. Boy, could he ever play the cello. He also was a great musical director and conductor. Sweetest man you'd ever want to know."

"All right, I give up," I laughed, "how on earth did you come to possess his, err, ashes?" "It was Shepard's wish to be cremated, and his family respected his wish. However, when his remains arrived at the post office to be picked up, no one could bring themselves to go. It was too gruesome. So Shepard's niece, remembering our friendship, called and asked if we'd like to have them. We'd be honored, we told her."

He's in most of our flower pots and the rest of him is here in this tin that he came in," Bob said as he pried off the lid and showed me what was left of their famous friend.

"Now come see my bedroom," Henry beckoned. Charmed by his eagerness, again I queued up for the remainder of the tour. Henry's room stood on the right front corner of the second floor. Built into the wall were two niches about a foot and a half deep. In one was displayed a large set of water buffalo horns behind Henry and his brothers' antique bottle collection. One night the horns rocketed across the room without knocking over any of the bottles. "If I'd been in bed, I would have been gored," Henry proudly announced. "Also, about once a year, I hear the low mumbling of men's voices coming from our dining room. It sounds like they're playing cards. Ginny Wrenchen said she used to hear them too."

"Getting back to our bottle collection," Bill took the conversation baton, "we've found every one of them while gardening in our yard."

"Some of them are labeled Dr. Jayne's Expectorant," Bob added. "It was Dr. Jayne who built this house in 1884. He lived here all of his adult life along with several servants whose quarters were on the third floor. Our neighbor to our left claims every once in a while to see a hazy light in our attic and people's shadows milling around. We've never used our attic. Do you think the shadows belong to the spirits of Dr. Jayne's servants?"

"Oh, we've found all kinds of things: arrowheads, pottery, and many animal skeletons including a wild boar. When we replaced the basement floor we even found a child's pair of slippers neatly tucked in a corner with some religious artifacts," Bill added.

After listening to their wealth of stories, I realized the triplets' home is a burial ground where objects and scents continue to circle through its rooms like debris orbiting through space forever. Unable to bear the airless rooms any longer, I thanked my new friends for an adventurous afternoon and rushed down their front stoop into the world of the living.

Before getting into my car I turned to look at the house. It seemed dark and abandoned, not at all like the home of three lively men who celebrate their lives with memorabilia and stories galore. Even the white, satin curtains now looked gray and dingy. For a split second I wondered if Bob, Bill, and Henry Aldinger were ghosts themselves. Wouldn't that be somethin'?

Mr. Skeleton

Christine Cole Pen & Ink

The Waterbury House Ghosts

My bedroom was on the third floor directly across from the entrance to the attic. The plank flooring had warped with age, which caused my door to remain ajar, leaving me a constant view of the hallway and the attic door from my bed. The attic terrified me and I used to hurry past its door into my room. Yet, once inside I was barely comforted. If you think that this was merely a child's ordinary fear of eerie places, you're mistaken. It was caused by a chilling encounter that I will remember for the rest of my life.

This story was told to me by Kimberly Merritt-Salido who lived in the Rowlee House out on Waterbury Road in the Edenville hamlet of Warwick from 1970 through 1977. Heman Rowlee built this stone house in 1790 for himself, his wife, and their ten children. After a century of ownership, the Rowlee family sold the house to James Waterbury. Waterbury was the owner who built the large wooden addition on the stone home's left side.

According to Mildred Parker Seese in her book, "Old Orange Houses," Waterbury's daughter Almeda was given a grand wedding in the home's maple grove one summer midnight in 1886. It was there that she married Charles Williams of the village of Florida. Their wedding was remembered throughout Edenville as elaborate and fanciful with lush festoons of flowers and Chinese lanterns. Later the newlyweds draped their nuptial garlands over rafters in the attic and there they remained for 100 years, until Pamela and Vernon Merritt converted the attic into their master bedroom.

In the far, right-hand corner of the attic stood a large steel mesh cage with a wooden frame. I was always told that the Rowlee family had installed it to cage either their daughter or a daughter-in-law who had lost her mind upon hearing that her husband was killed in the Revolutionary War. It was she who I believe I saw that night when I was twelve.

My sister Blaine was four and was temporarily sleeping in my room while hers was being renovated. One night she woke me with her crying. I looked at the clock on the nightstand and it was after one a.m. The last thing I remember was seeing my mother sitting on the edge of her bed trying to soothe her back to sleep. I woke up again, unaware that I had fallen back asleep after seeing my mom, and looked out into the hall. In the moonlight streaming in from the windows, I saw a dark shadow — a distinct, yet faint bodily outline of a woman standing in my doorway. I thought it was my mom waiting to make sure my sister had gone back to sleep. I called out to her, but she didn't answer. I looked at the clock again and saw that it was now four a.m. Immediately, I realized that my mother must have left the room hours ago. Again I looked toward the doorway to see the shadowy, unsubstantial outline of a woman. The long hair that hung over her shoulders and arms and down to her waist meant that she couldn't possibly be my mother. Mom's hair was short. After a brief moment, the figure simply moved from my line of sight and I could see the attic door again.

I was completely paralyzed with fear. Unable to call out or move, I lay dead still until well after sunrise. I was utterly terrified to be in that room after that. I couldn't bear that my door wouldn't close and that I would always be just on the other side of that attic door. For a long time, I wouldn't go up to my bedroom unless someone walked me.

I never had another experience, just creepy feelings. However, one of my mother's friends witnessed a different encounter. She drove into our driveway early one evening. It was dusk. The front of the house faced the road and there was an old stone hitching post on the right as you walked up to the double doors. Mom's friend vividly recalls seeing a soldier dressed in a red and white Revolutionary War uniform standing by the hitching post. As quickly as he appeared, he was gone. Maybe he was the husband of the wretched wraith who lived out her days locked in a cage in the attic like a character from Jane Eyre.

Another time, a pair of elderly women came to our door. They introduced themselves as two of the Davenports who grew up in the house around the turn of the last century. The house and property was then called The Davenport Stock Farm. There had been a huge stock barn to the right of the house that had burned down long before we lived there. A smaller barn now sat on part of its foundation. My mother invited them in and gave them a tour of the house. She revealed that she often felt a presence in the house and asked if they ever experienced anything supernatural. They both nodded saying they'd had many sightings, mostly of a man whom they believed to have been the handy man who lived in the basement when they were young children. He had passed away in his room, but the sisters continued to see him on numerous occasions, sometimes in the basement and sometimes on the third floor in the room that was to become my brother, Kip's, bedroom.

They also came upon a young boy from time to time. It was rumored that one of the Waterbury children had been killed in a horseback riding accident on the property. They surmised that the child they saw was he.

The women recounted how, when they were packed to move, their mother stood in the middle of the living room, surveyed its emptiness, and sighed saying, "In all the years we've lived here, I can't believe I never saw a ghost." The sisters stared at their mother with disbelief. If only she had known what they had seen over the years. And what's still being seen.

Oney's House

There it stood nestled on a curve of Sanfordville Road, resting against soft hills and meadows with a stream babbling just outside what was to become her office window. Oney Huffman, a tall, thin woman with a pretty face and long honey-blond hair, knew this was to be her home even before she and her husband, Huff, and their three children walked through its front door. It was everything she wanted — an old house in desperate need of restoration. Typical of the valley's vernacular farmhouses built in the late nineteenth century, it wasn't magnificent, but it exuded a cozy charm with its maze of hallways and erratic floorboards.

One fall afternoon Oney looked up from her desk and saw a long-haired, black cat in the meadow watching her through the window. He was a thin farm cat, probably homeless, who might have welcomed her acknowledgement as an invitation. However, he remained aloof.

At the sight of the cat, the floor creaked over her head as though someone walked across the room above her. Her children were in school and her husband was at work. Almost certain she'd find that one of her house cats had just hopped down from the bed, she climbed the stairs to make sure. Nothing was out of place, yet the room teemed with an eerie energy. And none of her cats lounged in its recesses. She returned to work, puzzled.

The following day, the cat appeared again with the same yellow-eyed stare. Oney looked at him thoughtfully. Although his stare was unsettling, he looked like he needed saving, like an old house, like her old house. The next day the black cat resumed his post. Again, Oney heard footfalls cross the bedroom above her office. Was the cat an omen that signaled the sound of the phantom footsteps? During the weeks that followed the cat and the footsteps continued to materialize simultaneously. Sometimes the footsteps were so loud that she had to ask her clients to stay on the line while she checked to see if someone had broken into the house. One day she was so convinced of an intruder that she called her husband at work and made him come home. He discovered exactly what she always had. Nothing.

Then there were the stove incidents. Oney began her restoration by replacing the kitchen appliances. The first stove didn't heat up when she turned it on, yet was often on full blast when she returned home from an errand. Being both mechanical and conscientious, she knew she hadn't left the burners on. She exchanged the stove for another. The same bizarre malfunctions occurred. She exchanged it for another, and another, and another. Now on her fifth stove, she shrugs that it still doesn't work properly.

During the months that followed, a long string of singular and isolated events occurred — none of which was alarming — unless you looked at them as a whole. Two cars drove through the white picket fence that graces the front yard (the second immediately after the fence had been repaired from the first, of course), the septic tank exploded into the house, the new dishwasher shorted out, and the roof leaked and leaked and leaked.

Then on February twenty-third of the year 2000, the most horrendous incident imaginable occurred. The house caught fire. Thankfully no one was hurt, but Oney's new kitchen, her bedrooms, and almost everything she and her family owned were gone.

Now, a year later, after living in hotel rooms and rentals, Oney and her family have moved back. The renovations are complete. Instead of painting and wallpapering, she spends her free time gardening. She and her new cat, a long-haired, black one I might add, often sit on a meditative bench, she enjoying the fruits of her labors, and he the joy of her company.

Weird things still happen, Oney says, "Closet doors that usually have to be tugged over the new wall-to-wall carpeting suddenly appear wide open when no one else is home, and there are other things, but I refuse to focus on them." Determined to overcome whatever energy possesses the house, she has made it her home. She self consciously tosses her hair and laughs, "Maybe it's me who is possessed."

Did the bearer of the ghostly footfalls start the fire? Only God knows, and maybe Blackie, Oney's most recent adoptee.

My Tale

You've probably guessed by now that I'm a believer. While researching this book many people asked if I'd ever seen a ghost. The answer is, "Yes, I've had three ghostly encounters, one of which I will conclude this section with."

This sighting occurred at Homestead Village, a condominium complex on the east-side of the village of Warwick. I moved there in November of 1987. In 1990 my husband, Jimmy, joined me and we continued to live there until 1998. For the family who bought our unit from us, please don't worry, this sighting was a one-time occurrence where the spirit had a specific purpose before going to the other side.

I grew up in the Warwick Valley, in the village of Greenwood Lake. As a child I longed to live in the village on the other side of the mountain — Warwick. I loved its Oakland and Maple Avenues that were neatly lined with oak trees and large Victorian Queen Anne and shingle homes with wrap-around porches. It was then that I developed an appreciation for a time when clothes were more elegant, furniture lasted a lifetime, and houses that were made of real wood and had detailed, finishing touches that distinguished their builders as artisans.

Homestead Village didn't fall into my dream category, but it was a start and it allowed me to move to the much-coveted, other side of Mt. Peter. When I moved in, the complex had only been completed up to my building. There weren't any streetlamps and the yards still hadn't been landscaped. It was easy to imagine that my neighbors and I were explorers setting up the first colony on the moon.

During those early months a camaraderie developed among us. My neighbors to my left were an older couple named George and Betty Mc Elroy. They were as tickled with their new place as I was. George had recently retired and he and Betty had sold the home where they brought up their children. They were excited to be starting this new, more leisurely chapter in their lives.

Our relationship soon developed into a friendship where we watched out for one another. When I was away they fed my cat Evelyn and when they were away I brought in their mail and newspapers. One afternoon when I was on my way in the front door George crossed the garden to speak to me looking worried. He asked, "Do you ever hear Betty crying at night?" I didn't want to embarrass him so I told him that I didn't. "Thank goodness," he sighed. "Betty suffers horribly from arthritis and she was worried she kept you awake."

Soon after our talk, Jimmy and I were married. It wasn't long before he became as attached to the Mc Elroys as I was. Betty's pain grew more fierce. Her doctors soon realized she wasn't suffering from a severe case of arthritis at all — she had bone cancer. George had a hospital bed installed in their dining room and nursed Betty himself at home.

From time to time he needed to ask Jimmy to help hoist her up in bed so she could eat. Jimmy was glad to do whatever he could. When he was nineteen he had lost his mother to brain cancer. He hadn't witnessed her suffering, because his family felt if he didn't go forward with his plan to enlist in the army his mother would realize that she was terminal. Two years later, he was summoned from Vietnam to her deathbed where his mother waited to see him one last time before passing on. Jimmy felt if he could help George care for Betty it would help heal the pain of knowing how his father cared for his mother by himself during the last years of her life.

Betty passed away in April of 1991. All of the families who lived on our street attended the services. Three nights after she died I woke to find myself sitting up in bed. Betty stood in front of me, just past our footboard. She wore a white gown that glowed with an ethereal light. "Betty, you look great," I said, astonished at my calmness. She smiled benevolently and responded, "I'm where I'm supposed to be. Just tell Jimmy I said thank you." With that she walked out of our bedroom and faded away at the top of the stairs.

I remained awake for a long time afterward, amazed at what had just happened and flattered that I was chosen to relay a message from beyond. I waited until the next morning to tell Jimmy of my otherworldly conversation, partly because I didn't want to wake him and partly because I wanted to keep the experience as my own for a little longer.

Later over breakfast I relayed Betty's message. Jimmy tearfully remarked, "You've given me back my belief in the afterlife."

TWO
HAUNTED INNS, SHOPS, AND FUNERAL PARLORS

The Staircase

Dancing at the Welling Hotel

Long ago, in the center of the village of Warwick stood an elegant, Second Empire style building called the Welling Hotel. Built in 1896, it was three stories tall with clapboard siding and a classic mansard, slate roof. Its two-tiered porch welcomed visitors by shading them from hot summer afternoons and cooling their conversations as darkness fell. The back of the building rambled for a block down Welling Place. Like so many of Warwick's old, large hotels, its tavern and dance hall were friendly meeting places for visitors and community members alike. Dances were held every weekend. They always began after seven, so the farmers could finish their workday and have a night on the town.

The tavern entrance was around the corner from Main Street on Welling Place. Inside was a long, narrow barroom with a dark staircase that led to the dance hall on the second floor. Young women in gingham dresses were often perched on the stairs as their suitors languidly leaned on the banister and chatted between square dancing sets. On Saturday nights the saw and twang of banjoes and fiddles could be heard all the way to Baird's Tavern.

During the 1930s, the hotel closed and a bakery and liquor store occupied the storefronts on either side of the main entrance. The rear barroom remained open and was called "Odell's." By 1945 the building fell into disrepair and was sold to the Warwick Telephone Company. The Telephone Company tore the hotel down and built the brick office building that stands there today. But some of the building's beams and boards were salvaged to build a new house around the corner on Elizabeth Street.

At that time Elizabeth Street only had one cape-style home on it. It was lived in by two life-long Warwick residents, whom we'll call Tim and Sally. They were newly married and worked long evenings at the Warwick Grange, often until midnight. Frequently, before pulling their car in the garage, they'd glance up at the new construction before going indoors.

One evening Tim went to work without Sally. When he arrived home, the newly framed house across the street was bustling with activity. He peered closer and saw the house crowded with shadow-like forms of people. They were square dancing. Tim decided he must have been more tired than he thought and went inside to bed. He didn't mention the dancers to Sally. A few nights later, when they were pulling into the garage, Sally exclaimed, "Look, the new house is full of people dancing!"

Tim and Sally saw the dancing specters several more times before the neighboring house's walls were completed. Did the boards of the old hotel harbor a memory that burst forth with its own energy every evening around midnight, or were they spirits who chose to spend their nights doing what they loved best — dancing at the Welling Hotel?

The Culver Randel Millhouse

You have only to look at its splendid Italianate-style architecture with its extravagant porch adorned with scrolled brackets and ornate balustrade to feel as though you've entered an American Gothic novel. Surrounded by formal gardens and oaks as old as fairytales, it sits on a rise on the other side of Quaker Creek from Route 94 as you drive into the village. Gold clapboards, creamy trim, and a wide paneled front door give it a grandness that could easily be imagined in the Deep South. The house is the Culver Randel Millhouse in Florida, New York.

Just across the creek stand the remains of the Randallville Mill. This portion of the building was built in 1830, however, the site was used by the Randel family for industrial purposes as early as 1740. Its four-story, narrow barn-like building has a unique idiosyncrasy, it lists to the right much like the Tower of Pisa, yet, the owners don't worry about it toppling. The building has been braced, so that it can keep its lean and still be structurally sound. Both of these buildings make up what used to be known as Randallville.

The millhouse was first built in 1790 and was remodeled and enlarged in 1845 by Culver Randel. It was Culver Randel who changed the spelling of the family sir name, which is Welch for "hill and vale," from "Randle" to "Randel." Later generations changed the spelling again to the current spelling of Randall. Culver used the mill buildings to manufacture pianos until the 1870s. He died at age 82 and passed the house and mill down to his son Jesse.

After Jesse's death twenty years later, no Randalls lived in Randallville until descendent Gary Randall and his wife Kathy bought the site in 1992. Recently retired from teaching, they threw themselves into a restoration project that has gained them stature on the National Register of Historic Places. They now use the mill and their home's basement for their antique shops. The house is beautifully refurbished with period furnishings that even include a piano made by Culver Randel.

As enticing as these buildings are with their showcase designs and rich local history, not everyone remembers them with amazement and appreciation. In fact, some people remember them with a spine-chilling horror.

On a sweltering Sunday in August, a couple whose names I can't reveal browsed through the antique shop in the mill. Gary Randall, always hospitable and proud of his heritage, gave them a tour of the building's second and third floors. The gentleman started to feel uneasy. When he crested the third floor, he read the words, "Ghosts are popular in this mill, so don't be surprised if you see J.R. and C.R. together," scrawled in chalk on the wall. Written in loopy cursive, it is characteristic of handwriting at the turn of the last century. Anxious and intrigued at the same time, he and his friend took up Gary's invitation to see more. They crossed the bridge over Quaker Creek and entered the shop's annex in the millhouse. They relaxed by asking Kathy more about the building's history. Because of their interest, she also invited them to tour the rest of the house.

As they climbed the worn pine stairs to the main floor, the gentleman blanched. He turned to his friend and asked, "Are you feeling what I'm feeling?" Astonished when she replied no, he exclaimed, "Look at me!" Goosebumps bristled from his arms. Then, the dark forms of several men swarmed around him. He couldn't make out their features or what they wore. Bodiless heads butted his shoulders. They yanked his clothing. They tugged his hair. "Stop it!" he blurted.

Unable to see what distressed her guest, Kathy continued the tour through the large parlors pointing out the marble fireplaces, plaster ceiling cornices and medallions, and family heirlooms. The couple then followed her to the second floor. "Go away! Go away I said," the man demanded as he jerked his arms away from the invisible grasps of a band of testy specters. "Are you all right?" his friend asked. "No," he gasped as he froze on the third step from the top. "Something horrible happened right here," he divined. "Do you know that this place is infested with spirits?" he asked Kathy in a voice that was somewhere between panic and accusation. Kathy remained composed and answered, "We may have one or two, but they're harmless. I like to think that they're pleased the house and mill are back in the family again." Refusing to go any further, he said, "Well, they're not pleased with me. I'm out of here," as he and his friend dashed down the stairs and out into the hot afternoon.

So far, no one else has been received in such a surly manner. The Culver Randel Millhouse and Randallville Mill are a treat along with their hosts, Kathy and Gary Randall, so do come and poke through their shops. But don't be surprised if something or someone pokes you back.

Baird Tavern

"A little closer, tha-a-t's it. Now a big smile for Francis," coaxed Jim Baird as he photographed Lynam Baird Freshour standing next to the cornerstone of the Francis Baird Tavern.

It was August 1, 1981 and 165 descendents of Francis Baird were flocking in from all over the United States for a gala long weekend at the Warwick Town Park. Lynam and his wife Edith had driven all the way from Mason, Michigan. This was the first Baird Family Reunion since 1910. Jim, son of Frieda and Leonard Baird of Bairdlea Farm in Sugar Loaf, had corresponded with the Freshours for almost a year in an effort to compile his genealogical research of the Baird Family. After months of research he had located and spoken to many relatives he never knew he had. Jim's project was met with enthusiasm and added many new chapters to the family history. What better way to celebrate the completion of his project than to throw a "Baird Reunion."

Lynam had never been to Warwick, but he knew it well through the slew of stories passed down from his father and grandfather. He was looking forward to meeting the many cousins he had heard about. Most of all, he was looking forward to meeting Jim, the distant cousin who had brought him to Warwick, the home of his ancestors.

When he and Edith arrived at the park they signed the guest book and picked up their nametags with the five-digit number that Jim had ingeniously assigned. The first two digits identified the number of generations the person was removed from Francis and Esther Baird, the first Bairds to have lived in Warwick. The next three numbers identified where that person fell within that generation. Lynam's number was 07058.

He spotted Jim right away, standing near one of the tables with the same handsome, finely chiseled face and striking smile worn by so many Bairds. Intuitively, Jim looked up and hurried over to give him and Edith a welcoming hug. Jim affectionately instructed them that they could not go back to Michigan without seeing the Baird Tavern.

Baird Tavern stands on the edge of the village of Warwick. It is its second oldest structure. Built in 1766, the limestone Dutch Colonial is now the home of The Warwick Historical Society and a major part of Warwick's legacy. It was built by none other than Francis Baird himself when he and his wife, Esther, and their young family first settled in Warwick. Francis was a merchant and book dealer from New York City. He purchased a 198-acre tract of land, which stood where Kings Highway forks with what used to be thought of as the Goshen Road and is now called "17A". It was the perfect location for a tavern because the road to the north connected the village to the nearest settlement and the road to the south went as far as Philadelphia.

The painted double doors on the left side of the front of the building lead into a large hall that was once a barroom. Behind the barroom was a keeping room. This room served as the living quarters for the Baird Family. Francis and Esther brought up their six children huddled around the fireplace in this cozy, cramped room.

Worn pine stairs lead to the second floor and attic. The second floor has two remarkable attributes. The front ballroom has a wooden partition hooked to the ceiling, which can be swung down to make two smaller rooms. According to Warwick author Jim Wright, only two other taverns in New York State from this era are known to have hinged walls. The other fact worth noting is that the floor to the ballroom is a "spring floor," which gave its dancers more bounce so they wouldn't tire as easily.

The two rooms at the back of this story served as bedrooms for the Baird Family and important guests, such as Martha Washington, who was one of the tavern's legendary lodgers.

There are two wooden framed additions on either side of the building. The southern addition was once used as a kitchen and general store, while the other served as a tailor shop, harness shop, tin shop, cabinetmaker's shop, and photography gallery.

Baird Tavern served locals and visitors alike for 64 years. Its most famous visitor was General George Washington on July 27th, 1782. According to history, toward the end of the Revolutionary War, Washington was returning to his headquarters in Newburgh after a meeting in Philadelphia with Count Rochambeau, head of the French forces in America. Accompanying him were two aides, Major Benjamin Walker and Colonel Jonathan Trumball Jr., brother of the American painter John Trumball. Reputedly, Walker paid two pounds, nineteen shillings and a six pence for their meals. Trumball paid nine shillings for their grog.

Later that afternoon, Lynam rode with Jim to see the legendary tavern. When they strolled around back Jim beckoned, "Let me take your picture by the cornerstone." It was inscribed "F. Baird, 1766." As Jim looked through the viewer of his camera, he noticed a figure other than Lynam in the frame. He peaked for an instant over the camera to see who had joined them. There was Francis himself, tall and skinny with dark hair nodding a most approving smile. Jim snapped the picture and quickly looked up to catch a second look, but the apparition had vanished.

Knowing what he'd just seen, Jim was certain his quest to bring his family together to celebrate their history had come to a fruition greater than he had ever imagined.

The Engagement Ring

In 1978 Joy Sprake and her husband Trevor bought what was once the Sugar Loaf Hotel and is now called "The Old Sugar Loaf Inn," for their home and business. Built by Edgar Litchult, the rambling building was around 225 years old and began as a bar, rooming house, and livery. After Litchult, Bill Seely owned the establishment and added a dance hall in the late 1830s. The hotel was active until The Depression, when it was left to molder into disrepair. In the early 1970s, the building was bought by the Henyczes, who repainted the white clapboard siding and repaired the front two-story porch. The Sprakes in turn bought the restored hotel from them and it was there that Joy opened her antique shop, Joy's Corner.

Joy suffered from migraines and was wracked with a terrible one on the sunny fall day when a dark-haired gentleman wearing navy blue trousers and a yellow, Izod windbreaker walked into her shop in search of a ring. With penetrating dark eyes, he had an odd look about him, yet she wasn't frightened. She asked if he needed any help. "Yes," he responded, "You have something of mine — a ring that I gave to my fiancée." Joy told him she didn't carry jewelry, only furniture. "But you phoned saying you have it," the man insisted, ignoring her comment as he began to hunt for the engagement ring. "You remember, the silver band with the small sapphire," he reminded.

He must have me confused with someone else, thought Joy, as she quietly tolerated his search through her sideboards and dressers. Next, the curious customer opened a drawer to one of her bird's-eye maple bureaus and took out a small, velvet jewelry box. Reaching in the box, he brought out the silver ring with the blue stone he had described. Joy then recalled coming across the velvet box when she purchased the bureau at an estate sale, but had since forgotten about it.

"Here it is!" he exclaimed. "My fiancée lost this a long time ago and has been looking for it ever since. Now she can rest in peace." He added, "Her father built this hotel." Knowing the building had been built in 1750, Joy began to think this was a practical joke. The man went on to tell her the hotel's history. Sensing he was accurate, she listened uneasily. He claimed that during the 1750s while he was courting Miss Mary Litchult, he always parked his buckboard wagon in front. "Now my wagon is in the back — buried under your garden," he said knowingly.

"How much is the ring?" the gentleman asked. "Forty dollars," Joy stated, thinking it was a fair price. "Oh, it's worth much more than that," he responded while reaching in the back pocket of his trousers for his wallet. By this time, Joy's head felt cinched with white pain that was as sharp as lightning and she grew impatient with the strange conversation. She insisted that her fee was reasonable. The man thanked her graciously. On his way out the door, he predicted, "From now on you won't wake up with a headache."

Joy walked gingerly to the front of the store to see where this mysterious man headed next. She peered up and down the street. He was nowhere in sight.

Later that evening, she laughed as she told Trevor about her odd morning. He asked, "Why don't we dig up the garden?" Joy cherished her English garden and everyone who knew her associated her with it. "Don't be ridiculous," she protested. "I've spent years on that garden." Trevor was determined, and Joy eventually gave in to his curiosity. They dug, and sure enough, they slowly uncovered the remnants of a wagon wheel that could well have been there for over 200 years.

There is another unexplainable end to this story. The strange visitor also gave Joy a wonderful gift in exchange for finding the ring of his beloved Mary; Joy has not had a migraine since their meeting twenty-five years ago.

The Peach Grove Inn

"We bought this house because we felt sorry for it," laughs Lucy Mastropierro, co-owner of the bed and breakfast known as the Peach Grove Inn. She and her husband John bought the handsome, Greek Revival Farmhouse in 1989 and are lovingly restoring it to its former splendor.

"Although it had all of its original moldings and few structural changes, it's an on-going project," Lucy sighs. It was two years before we were able to open our home to the public and, of course, the work continues."

As John and Lucy restore each room, the walls and floorboards reveal more and more of their home's history. Recently, they restored

Christine Cole Pen & Ink

a screened-in porch that runs the length of the rear of the building. After they peeled off three walls and ceilings of different materials and even a makeshift kitchen, the exhumed porch itself instructed them on how to finish it. Until then, they had planned to evenly space four Greek columns to support the roof, but the original pine plank floor marked where the former ones had stood and were placed differently. The center pillars were spaced dramatically wider than their distance from their corner mates. When the Mastropierros compared this spacing with the columns on the front porch, they discovered that the center ones were also spaced wider apart than the others to dramatize the entryway. Of course, they altered their plans.

The Peach Grove Inn's old timbers aren't the only things in the house with a history to tell; one of the bed and breakfast's guests has reported the appearance of a spirit whose past is not as easily unveiled. Did the restoration projects stir the spirit from eternal sleep or did the early mortar and boards release an energy that only reveals itself to the very sensitive? Whatever it was, Lucy and John have not yet met or even heard their non-paying guest.

A year after they opened their bed and breakfast, they received an intriguing letter from a woman named Lee who had recently stayed in the upper, left bedroom with her husband. Lee wrote that during her stay she experience two strange phenomena. She was awakened to discover a man in an old-fashioned nightshirt standing between her side of the bed and the armoire. He struck a match, lit a candle and peered curiously into her face. Then, a small terrier-like dog jumped onto the bed, scampered over her and her husband, and leaped off the other side. Both apparitions vanished as quickly as they appeared. Lee thought of waking her husband, but was too startled to move. She wrote in her letter that she wasn't frightened in retrospect, just curious whether anyone else had recounted a similar incident.

Lee's letter was not the first report of a presence. Shortly after Lucy and John hung out their sign, a small woman wearing a large hat with a posy in its center knocked on their door. She didn't need a place to stay, but instead asked if she could simply walk through to see what they had done with the place. Once inside the eight-foot tall, paneled red door, she walked past the parlors on either side and climbed the staircase in the majestic, two story front hall. When she complimented the faux marble walls, Lucy relayed how they duplicated the original technique that decorated the walls 150 years earlier. Smitten by their 1850 farmhouse's history and architecture, she and her husband have kept its stylistic subtleties even in their interior decorating. On the landing in front of one of the coffin niches, the woman in the floppy hat turned toward Lucy and John and announced, "You have a presence here, but you needn't worry — I can tell it's a happy one. I've been psychic all my life and grew up in a house with a ghost," she then confided. Lucy giggled. "We got a kick out of her assuredness. Since then a few other guests have reported a presence, but as far as we know, only Lee has met him in spirit, along with his dog!"

"We know that this house was built by Colonel William F. Wheeler as a wedding gift for his son, Isaac Van Duzer Wheeler, and his wife

Phebe A. Bull in 1850. Wheelers have lived in Warwick for generations," Lucy added. "In fact, William's father Joel was on the board that planned for the Baptist Meeting House to be built in the center of town."

Colonel Wheeler chose one of Warwick's most sophisticated builders, Brookes Parmley, to build his wedding gift. Parmley was already highly regarded for building for several other established families in Warwick including the Wisners and Belchers. He also built the miniature Greek Revival home in Bellvale now owned by Brian Singer, also a highly regarded carpenter in Warwick. Coincidentally, Singer is the contractor who has done most of our work."

Other stories have come to the Mastropierros about their stow-a-way specter. When the Higgins Family formerly owned the house, Eliana Higgins witnessed strange phenomena. Several times while she played with her toddler, Michelle, she observed that her baby smiled off in another direction as though someone else was there.

On another occasion, Eliana was in her bedroom when she heard the front door slam and footsteps walk through the front hall, up the stairs and into the bedroom overhead. Assuming it was her mother-in-law arriving home from work she quickly forgot about it, until her mother-in-law walked in later. "Did you come home earlier and go back out again?" she asked. "No," her mother-in-law responded, "I just got home." Eliana was certain she heard two arrivals and remembered that her dog, Rusty, barked on both occasions.

Who was the man in the nightshirt? Could it be the bridegroom Isaac Wheeler? "Until we see him ourselves," John and Lucy comment "we won't even speculate."

Gilvan's

The dark silhouette of a man flickered into Matthew's peripheral vision. Then a shadow darted behind a steel pillar and turned side-

ways out of view. "Who's there?" Matthew called. No one answered. Since he was alone in his furniture store, he closed the register before investigating. Again, he caught sight of a shadow as it leaped behind an armoire. This time Matthew quickly crept around the furniture displays to see if he could catch the intruder. This playful, "Now you see me, now you don't," continued as Matthew peaked around columns, over-sized couches and cabinetry. Each time he caught a quick glimpse, the person was in a different section of the building. No mortal could cross from one end of the large open floors to the other that swiftly. Matthew checked every corner of the four-story building to confirm what he already knew. Then, he locked up and went home, because he was sure that the person teasing him wouldn't steal anything. The intruder wasn't of flesh and blood.

Sound strange? Not after interviewing Matthew who seems to be embroiled in the building's history through some weird time phantasm, as though he's an embodiment of the builder, W.T. Anderson, himself. Several other shop owners who have rented space at 40 Main Street over the years have equally curious stories to tell.

When the building was first erected in 1890, the villagers referred to it as "Anderson's Folly" because Anderson built his department store on an ancient graveyard site.

In retrospect, his venture was more brazen than foolish and he flaunted it by choosing majestic, gothic architecture. Surrounded by older, clapboard sided, Colonial storefronts, his building stands out as the most elaborate and imposing building in the village to this day. From its slate tiled roof, symmetrical pairs of false chimneys guard the corners of its façade like sentinels. Ecclesiastical peaks, arches, and windows connect the chimneys. At dusk when clouds glide across their whiskey-tinted glass, the church-like windows that line the top story take on the appearance of tombstones.

Anderson proved himself a good merchant by opening Orange County's largest department store where he sold everything from groceries to dry goods that even included fur coats. He gave Warwick the convenience of shopping for necessities and fineries that ordinarily could only be purchased in nearby cities.

After being sold several times, the store became known as Gilvan's Clothing Store in 1963. Gilvan's continued to provide the town with personal service and quality merchandise. And although it has been sold a few times since then, it continues to be known as "The Gilvan's Building."

In 1992, Mike Myrow leased the building to five businesses, creating a small indoor shopping mall on the basement and first floor. The first merchant to set up her store on the main floor asked that I not use her real name or her daughter's, so I will refer to them as Vivian and Lisa. Whenever she used the building's only bathroom at the rear of the second floor, she had the eerie feeling that she wasn't alone. One morning Lisa bolted out of the bathroom in a panic. She was certain she felt someone brush past her as she opened the door. Vivian admitted that she also frequently felt an intrusive presence in the bathroom. But that wasn't all. She asked Lisa if she noticed how various pieces of furniture stored on the second floor were positioned differently each morning than they had been the evening before. She called Mr. Myrow to ask if perhaps he lent the space for community meetings in the evenings. He assured her he didn't.

Intrigued, Lisa jumbled the furniture before they closed on several evenings. Morning after morning, the chairs were repositioned to face one another. Who was there after hours? How many? And why?

One snowy November afternoon when business was slow, Vivian and Lisa explored the attic. The back staircase was a mass of fuse boxes and crumbling plaster. Cobwebs tore across their faces. They opened the door to a huge room bathed in wintry, gray light from the tombstone-shaped windows. The room was cluttered with antique light fixtures, steamer trunks of old clothing, and various remnants left by former owners and tenants. When they opened a lid to one of the trunks, both women felt as though they were about to be caught rummaging through someone else's belongings. The clothing teamed with an overpowering energy from past owners. Their hearts raced as they fled down the back stairs to their shop. They knew they had trespassed.

Unable to resist, Lisa continued to brave the attic. After a while she felt safe enough to try on the old clothes provided she didn't take them. She particularly enjoyed wearing a sealskin top hat.

Years later, during the bustle of the holidays, Lisa's friend Tom stopped in to tell her and her mom that he had volunteered to drive a horse and buggy around town to help draw Christmas shoppers to the village. He asked if they had an old hat he could borrow to complete his Dickensian garb. Lisa remembered the hat in the attic and, forgetting her unspoken agreement, loaned it to Tom. He returned within the hour. Spooked. He handed the hat back to her saying, "Something tells me I'm not supposed to wear this."

In October of 1995, a woman we'll call Holly moved her store into Gilvan's. Whenever she walked up the back staircase to the second floor, she passed through cold layers of air. She also felt as though she was intruding into someone's private quarters. She didn't mention these feelings to Vivian, who had been so supportive of her starting her own business and had become a good friend.

Diligent to get her new business off the ground, she often worked late into the night on her bookkeeping. Each evening around nine thirty, Holly heard a radio playing 1940s ballroom music. She wondered if it was a childish prank because of the overwhelming feeling she was being watched. Twice she got up from her desk and searched the building for a radio that might have been left on. She crept down the basement stairs and pressed her ear against the partition to another shopkeeper's bookstore. The music stopped. When she returned to her desk, it resumed. Women giggled. When she searched other parts of the building, the giggling grew louder. Holly refused to be driven out and went back to her desk to continue working.

Every evening that she worked late, Holly heard women's light banter and giggling and dealt with it by acknowledging her hosts. "Okay, ladies you're scaring me now. I'm making your space beautiful, so please let me do my work." The female specters would quiet down, but it was an eerie silence. By 11:00 a cold chill blanketed the building. Holly learned intuitively to pack up and go home before this hour.

Vivian and Holly continued their friendship after they moved their shops elsewhere in town. One evening the topic of ghosts came up and Vivian said, "I'm certain the Gilvan's Building is haunted by former owners and clerks." Stunned, Holly relayed her experiences. They couldn't believe neither of them had ever confided these incidents before.

In 1997, The Gilvan's Building was sold again and leased to one business on its main and second floors. Colleen leased the upper floors for her home décor store, Home Front America. Her brother, Matthew, helped open the store and stayed on as her display artist and partner. He often worked till morning creating faux painted backdrops for his various furniture and bed and bath arrangements. "I always felt someone with me," Matthew reports, "It was a friendly presence and I believed that whoever it was liked what I was doing."

One evening Matthew returned to the store to retrieve something he'd forgotten earlier during his shift. A golden light bathed the first floor. Out of the corner of his eye, he saw a woman primly sitting in a wingback chair. She was wearing a black uniform a store clerk may have worn during the early twentieth century. Thin with dark hair, blue eyes, and an aristocratic nose, she smiled off in the distance looking very satisfied and pleased with herself. She seemed to be savoring the comfort of the chair. As Matthew watched her, the lines from *My Fair Lady's* "Wouldn't It Be Loverly?" flashed through his mind: "All I want is a big fine chair/far away from the cold night air./ Wouldn't it be loverly?" When he reached the refrain, the woman vanished.

Like Vivian, Lisa, and Holly before him, Matthew reports the same oppressive feeling in the attic. He keeps damaged pieces of furniture there until he has a chance to repair them. Once, when he went to fetch a broken ladder-back chair, he discovered it set up in front of a corner window. When he looked out the window, much to his disconcertment, the chair was perfectly angled to give its occupant a view across the rooftops into his apartment. Matthew had reckoned with the spirits in the building and even felt a kinship with them, but he didn't want them to cross over into his outside life.

Long before he knew Warwick existed, he had a recurring dream about Gilvan's and the catacomb-like tunnels that connect it to other stores. The tunnels really exist and once facilitated the Underground Railroad. Some people have remarked how he resembles builder W.T. Anderson, himself, pictured on the historic plaque on the front of the building. For these reasons, and a steady accumulation of new ones, Matthew's certain he's somehow connected with the spirits who watch over him there.

Are the spirits from the disturbed graves beneath the building or are they former owners and employees whose ephemeral outlines are eternally seared into modern times? Has Matthew been sent back to repeat his work in the Gilvan's building to learn why he's been given life on earth? Anything is possible when you open yourself to the possibility of ghosts.

The employees of Home Front America have become quite blasé about their spirits. Recently, Matthew whispered to Tara, a coworker, that he just saw one of the ghosts standing in the corner of the water closet. "Oh, he was there yesterday," was her reply.

The New Milford Country Store

"... suddenly there came a tapping, As of some one gently rapping — rapping at my chamber door,"
Edgar Allan Poe

Warwick's general stores are still a good stop for a tale or two, but only the New Milford Country Store and Post Office reverberates with a ghostly energy. Owned by Caroline and Mark Monteverdi, the store is a nostalgic treat with its homemade soups and desserts.

Mark became the store's owner in 1991 and has lived in an apartment upstairs ever since. In 1997, he was joined by his wife Caroline. The couple lives there today with their son Zachary.

A week after Caroline moved in, she was alone in their apartment when she heard a knocking in the bathroom wall. She was in a hurry to open the store and dismissed the sound as water pipes clanging. Clang, bang, tap, CRASH!!! The sound persisted. Spooked, she escaped downstairs without blowdrying her hair. Later, she asked Mark if he had ever heard noises in the bathroom wall. "All the time," he assured her, "it happens because it's an old building." She then felt silly for having fled their apartment earlier that morning.

Caroline learned more about the Warwick Valley as she got to know the store's steady customers. One woman shared that she had rented the other apartment on top of their shop when she first came to the States as an exchange student. "Did you ever hear unexplainable banging in the walls or someone walking in rooms you were certain were empty?" Caroline asked. "Yes," the woman giggled, "I always believed this building was haunted."

Despite her husband's rational explanations, Caroline's curiosity was peaked. Intrigued, she strove to learn more about the building's history. The more she learned about the New Milford area, the more enchanting and mysterious it became. Months after she felt familiar enough with a lifelong resident who neighbored the store, she asked if anything traumatic ever happened in their building.

The woman hesitated a moment. "Well, you probably already know the original general store burned down in the New Milford Fire in 1902." Caroline had heard that, but it didn't answer whose spirit might be walking her halls at night. "There were rumors," the neighbor continued, "that the fire was arson. People thought the owner had misappropriated federal funds from his post office, but nothing was ever proven and as far as I know no one died in the fire." "Anything else?" Caroline coaxed. Searching her memory, the neighbor continued, "During the 1940s and '50s a married couple named Clint and Marion Edsall owned this store. Marion outlived Clint and tried to make a go of the country store on her own. She was an attractive woman with graying hair who looked much younger than her fifty-eight years. Her neighbors thought of her as an educated woman who was kind and pleasant to talk to."

One morning Marion didn't open the store on time. Her neighbor who rented the small building on the side for her antique store became concerned. She went upstairs and knocked on Marion's door to see if she was ill. When she didn't answer, she walked in and called her name. Marion's body was lying in the bathtub. She was believed to have slipped and hit her head on the tub's porcelain edge as she lowered herself into the water the previous evening."

Caroline Monteverdi feels Marion's untimely death explains the racket that often occurs in her bathroom wall and the phantom heels that click through her kitchen and living room at night. Marion Edsall's traumatic death has kept her forever rapping in the very bathroom that took her life.

Surrealist Secret

We are about to stroll down the slate path toward the Seligmann Homestead Museum in Sugar Loaf, New York. Let yourself be lulled by the pastoral 55-acre farm. Stone-tiered, formal gardens surround the idyllic center hall colonial, circa 1760, with its neat brown clapboards and black shutters. If you don't know anything about the farm's former owner, you probably think you are about to walk back in time into one of Orange County's well-restored eighteenth century farmhouses. And you are. But the reason for this tour is not so much for your enjoyment of its restoration as it is for the amazement of learning who once lived here. This museum is a remembrance of the late Kurt Seligmann, an internationally famous surrealist painter and his wife, Arlette, who bequeathed their home and studios for our pleasure and education ... some say for its mystery as well. Seligmann was the first Paris-based Surrealist to relocate to New York before the outbreak of the Second World War.

Before I bring you inside the hand-hewn, sienna door, open yourself up to the possibility of spotting Seligmann himself sitting on the small porch smoking his pipe. By closing your eyes, you may hear his intellectual banter with the thin, rumple-haired Marcel Duchamp. Let me bring you back to the year 1946, four years after the Seligmanns settled in this rural hamlet just outside the Warwick Valley. On the step below them sits the French poet, Andre Breton, who founded Surrealism. While gathered on the lawn sitting cross-legged are the painters Fernand Leger, Yves Tanguy, Max Ernst, and Piet Mondrian, the sculptors Hans Arp and Alexander Calder, the gallery owner Peggy Guggenheim, and the art historian Meyer Schapiro. Later tonight, Seligmann will amaze us in his barn studio with one of his magic shows.

Try not to stare, as they thrive on not being recognized. As we enter the front hall, savor the aroma of Arlette Seligmann's cooking. She's in the primitive, lean-to kitchen sautéing her garden vegetables in the greasy wrought iron fry pan she was often chided about. She's about to toss them into a serving bowl bedecked with a silver ladle, and place them on the dining room table alongside a large slab of bread, cheese, and red wine for her and her husband's guests.

Shall we fade into the background of the left parlor and watch them while they dine? Real ghosts they may not be, well all except for one, but the energy of the Seligmanns and their stellar friends can be felt throughout the house. This is the only room still furnished with the Seligmann's European antiques, belongings, and famous paintings that vibrate with esoteric energy. With their armor and helmets, ribbons, feathers, and bones, the painting's haunting figures seem to preside over the room. According to Martica Sawin, author of *Surrealism in Exile,* Seligmann, like the other Surrealists, tempted to explore those areas of the human psyche where the propensity for violence lurked.

In retrospect, Seligmann's paintings foreshadowed the atrocities of the Second World War, using a dark mysteriousness distinctly his own. He used Occult symbolism from his vast research into magic, the Tarot and the supernatural for his book, *The History of Magic and the Occult*. A viewer doesn't have to be a scholar in the Occult to feel disturbed when looking at his paintings, although Seligmann's goal was not to intimidate, but to record humanity's efforts to reconcile the opposing forces of Good and Evil within the individual and society.

Hanging alongside his paintings are photographs of himself: one at age five dressed in a clown outfit and holding a hoop in his hometown of Basil, Switzerland, in 1910; and a much later photo of him, bespectacled and wearing forties-style, pleated trousers in his Paris studio.

The dinner conversation has turned to whom Seligmann is arranging to bring to the United States next. From dusty offices, he's arranged the necessary paper work and affidavits for many of his colleagues, including a few sitting in front of us around the table. Max Ernst is talking about the Tarot and how their friend, Salvador Dali, is designing his own deck. Arlette sits stately and quietly, listening to her husband speak. She is used to such settings. Being the niece of Georges Wilderstein, an international art dealer, she grew up in similar surroundings. Arlette has been instrumental in seeing that these artists' works are shown throughout Europe.

Now, let's leave our imagined hosts and tour the second floor. This is the caretaker's quarters and is usually not open to the public. The staircase is early twentieth century, which undoubtedly replaced the original staircase in the same location as the present one, only with a steeper rise. As we crest the top of the stairs, notice the slanted hallway that wraps around the open banister.

I must warn you that this is the moment when many men have become rattled and excused themselves from this tour. Here, an oppressive presence envelopes them. It hovers over them until they can no longer stand it and have to leave. None of the women who have walked through this farmhouse have ever felt what these men describe.

Kurt Seligmann died from an accidental gunshot wound to the head in 1962. Because so many artists during this era committed suicide, the circumstance of his death has always been questionable.

Some people believe Seligmann's spirit still looks out for Arlette who survived him by over thirty years. He had a reputation for being protective of his petite wife and his ghost may be still be leery of other men in his home. Or perhaps he has stayed on to watch over the museum's caretaker, who is the current lady of the house.

If anyone can cross back and forth between the spiritual world and our own, we would have to give this distinction to the conjurer and artist himself, Kurt Seligmann.

The Exorcism

As you can imagine, having handled dead people for years, I'm not easily spooked. I've performed over 1,900 funerals in this building and until this incident nothing unexplainable has ever happened. I would prefer that our names be changed because this story is painful to those who lived it.

When our daughters, Megan and Becky, were school age, Faith and I bought a 100-year-old Queen Anne shingle-style house in Orange County, New York. It was a sprawling Victorian with asymmetrical turrets and towers and steep gables reminiscent of medieval England. In retrospect, it was the perfect house for a haunting.

We converted the downstairs into my funeral home and the second and third floors into a twelve-room apartment for the four of us. Soon after we moved in, we became friendly with our neighbor, Chris, who lived across the street. Chris was a single mother with two pretty, blond teenage daughters named Anna and Judith. We often hired them to babysit our girls. Chris also cared for her Polish parents, Agnes and Stanley, who lived in a separate apartment in her house.

Whenever we noticed the older couple, Chris's father seemed to be fuming about something. He was a white-haired gentleman with hunched shoulders and an angry fixed expression. We'd see him shuffling around the yard muttering to himself. He didn't speak English and pined for his homeland. He and Agnes never seemed happy. Maybe we read this into it later. I'm not sure.

One evening we came home late to the phone ringing. It was Chris. She stammered, "My father hanged himself. Please come help me!"

The family had gone to visit relatives and Stanley chose to stay behind. When they came home and pressed the garage door opener, they were faced with his dangling body.

I rushed over, cut Stanley down and brought him to the morgue, which was in the downstairs of our home. Besides being a funeral director, I was also the county medical examiner's assistant. Faith went over and tried to comfort Anna and Judith who were, of course, in shock. The whole thing was awful. It was the most tragic death I've ever encountered.

During the viewing hours no one in the family would look at the casket. They actually turned their chairs around to face the back of the room. No one spoke or looked at one another except for Anna and Judith who repeatedly asked, "If Grandpa had to kill himself, why did he have to do it that way?"

As time went by, we noticed some odd things going on in our home. It's hard to explain — but everyone who lives in a building knows that buildings make noise: the heat goes on, the shutters rattle when the wind blows, the pipes clang, and the floors creak. After you live in a place for a while, you discount these sounds because you know your home's idiosyncrasies. It's when these sounds are out of sync that you think twice about them. And being rational human beings most of us say, "Oh well, it's just my imagination." But in our case, these things kept going on until we had to say, "Now wait a minute. There is something funny going on here."

We'd remember turning out the lights before we went out and find them on when we returned. We'd hear the heat roar on in July. Doors slammed in areas of the house we were certain were empty. Then the main light switch in the hall of the third floor stopped working all together.

Later that summer two incidents occurred which really convinced me we had a ghost. The first was our girls started having nightmares and saying there's a man trying to get us. Becky insisted there was a man outside their second story window who was trying to break in. We hadn't told them how their babysitter's grandfather died, and had no idea what was frightening them until one night when Megan came in our room crying. She sobbed, "There's a man standing in our bedroom with a rope around his neck. He keeps saying, 'Come with me.'" Faith asked Meg to describe the man. "He's an old bent man with white hair," she sputtered.

The second disturbance occurred when we were awakened by a loud clanging noise coming from downstairs in the Preparation Room. It was the chilling sound of one of the stainless steel buckets slamming against the porcelain tiles that line the room. Certain that someone was downstairs, we called the police. I asked them to wait outside while I crept from room to room turning on lights, hoping to flush the intruder out the front or back door. I went through the whole house and found no one. The police didn't find any signs of a break in. After they left, Faith and I looked at each other and asked, "What the hell is going on?"

For weeks, Faith had been telling me there was an evil spirit in our house. She had a recurring dream that a phantom energy was trying to smother her. Her heart would race, and she would try to scream, but would be unable. She'd force herself awake, to find herself covered in perspiration. Whenever she shut her eyes to go back to sleep, she was haunted by a hideous red glow and a paralyzing pressure on her chest that made her panic for air.

"What should we do?" we pleaded with one another. I thought of a priest whom I trusted wouldn't laugh at our story and sent for him immediately.

He explained that it was common for a person who commits suicide to think that his or her misery will end when he succeeds in ending his life. However, during his years in the priesthood he found that a person's spirit continues to be miserable unless it can come to some acceptance or closure. He reassured us that this was not the first call he'd received of this kind. We followed him through every room in the building while he prayed reverently for Stanley's spirit to be released and go in peace.

From that time on, we never had another disturbance; however, the light switch on the third floor still doesn't work. We've hired countless electricians to repair it and they are unable.

THREE

HAUNTED RESTAURANTS

The Dining Room Table

Christine Cole

THE BARNSIDER TAVERN

The Ghost in the Tweed Suit

Cheryl Kannon, co-owner of The Barnsider Tavern, first saw their ghost one evening when she and her husband Matthew were closing the restaurant. As she walked out of the kitchen and climbed the steps into the small corridor leading to the barroom, she saw a man standing before her. Used to seeing all kinds of people daily, she didn't find it unusual and only noticed that he was a middle-aged gentleman with brown hair wearing a dark brown tweed suit — the type a farmer would wear on Sunday. Or be buried in. "I'm sorry sir," she said, "the bar is closed." With the blink of her eye, the man vanished. Cheryl knew instinctively she had just seen the spirit whose presence was felt by many of the waitresses. During late nights around the bar, they often told ghost stories. Inevitably, someone always admitted, "I think we have one here."

Cheryl rushed into the barroom to be with Matt as he finished setting the burglar alarms. Nervously, she continued to the front of the tavern to busy herself with the routine of setting tables for the following day. Matthew's concentration was broken by someone wavering beside him. Assuming it was Cheryl, he said, "Hold still." When he looked up, the person he saw was hardly his wife. Instead, he caught sight of half of a man's head on top of one shoulder with an arm clothed in a dark tweed jacket before it disappeared. Afraid to mention what he'd seen in its presence, he hurriedly finished his task, called Cheryl and locked up. Before they left the parking lot, Cheryl announced, "I saw the ghost tonight." Matt stuttered, "Oh my God, so did I." When they exchanged stories, they discovered the only similarity was the dark tweed jacket. Until then, no one had ever reported an actual sighting.

The following spring, Cheryl saw the same suited gentleman standing in the staff locker room. Again, he disappeared instantly. Even though she had seen him once before, she was shaken. "I didn't realize how remarkable the encounter was until immediately afterward," recalls Cheryl.

Later that evening another strange disturbance occurred. Before locking up, she turned the exhaust fans off in the kitchen. As she left the building, she heard their roar. Thinking she must have hit the wrong switch, she darted back in to turn them off. This time she waited as their warm drafty hum spun to a stop. On her way out the door, she heard them again. Once more, she flipped the fans off and ran out the front door. Again the fans whirred. Too spooked to try to turn them off again, she raced home. To this day she believes their visitor in the tweed suit was teasing her.

A Recurring Calamity

The appearance of the man in the tweed suit was not the first incident that alarmed Cheryl in The Barnsider. In 1990 when she moved in with Matt in his apartment above the restaurant, she had a strange dream. It was of the hamlet of Sugar Loaf as it must have looked in the early 1800s. The village's main street was a dirt road.

Cheryl saw herself walking down the hill toward what is now the post office. She passed a man leading oxen. She heard horses come up quickly behind her. When she turned, she saw the horses pulling a buckboard with a couple dressed for church. Church bells were ringing. Something startled the horses and they bolted as they rounded the curve on the hill. The buckboard hurled on its side, flinging its passengers into the street. Cheryl could see that the couple was badly hurt. She wanted to help them, but was too distraught. Just then, she was awakened by the touch of a man's hands as they slid down each side of her body and the covers descended to the bottom of the bed. She sprung up with her heart pounding. No one was there. She had the eerie feeling that whoever or whatever it was that stole her and Matthew's covers had come from their bedroom closet. For the rest of the night, she lay watching the closet doors just beyond the foot of their bed.

The following evening Cheryl and Matt brought home a puppy. His first night was spent barking outside the same closet door. Cheryl opened the door repeatedly to show the puppy and herself that there was nothing to fear. Did the puppy sense what she had the evening before?

Later that week, Cheryl told her mother-in-law about her eerie dream. "That's the 'Calamity Corner' story," she exclaimed. "The curve on King's Highway where Sugar Loaf's main street forks into Pine Hill Road has been nicknamed Calamity Corner for hundreds of years, because of the number of accidents that have occurred there. Your dream is similar to the original tale that gave the curve its nick name."

Cheryl was astounded.

During this interview, I asked if she remembered what the man was wearing in her dream who was thrown from the wagon. As she responded, "A dark woolen suit," she paused realizing what I suspected.

Could the spirit who occasionally appears in The Barnsider belong to the man who was killed on "Calamity Corner" over 200 years ago? If the tweed jacket fits, I believe he's wearing it.

The Sugar Loaf Inn

In her small cottage surrounded by abundant English gardens, her paintings, family, and pets galore, Gail Link tells the story of

"Marty," the resident ghost of her restaurant known as the Sugar Loaf Inn. She and her husband, Bruce Fisher, bought the 200-year-old inn in 1981.

The building was used for many things, Gail recounts. In 1900, it was owned by the Van Duzer family and was used as a general store and post office. Later it became a grain depot and then a farmers' Grange Hall. It sunk into disrepair and disuse from time to time. The owners before us, the Ludlows, were the first people who used the building for their private home. They restored the building from top to bottom and some of their touches seemed to uncannily prepare for our family's ownership.

We were looking for a farmhouse that could easily be turned into a restaurant on the first floor and an apartment for us on the second. When we saw that the Ludlows had already installed an apartment on the second floor, we were certain the building was meant to be ours.

On the day Bruce and I moved in with our son, Robin, we immediately felt a spiritual presence. Our every move was watched by unseen eyes. Chills ran up our spines whenever we sliced vegetables, set the tables, or washed the dishes. In fact, no matter what we did, we'd catch ourselves looking up and feel silly when no one was there. Then one night as I baked in the basement kitchen after hours, I saw him. I felt someone move past me. When I looked up, I saw a tall, thin man with dark hair wearing a white ruffled shirt and black pants. He headed toward a dead-end section of the hall. Shivers raced up my spine as I coaxed myself to stay to finish the next day's pies.

This was not my first haunting. As a child I often spent weekends and summers with my aunt and uncle in their old farmhouse in Florida, New York. That's when I fell in love with this area, despite that I was certain their house was haunted. Before tucking me in each night, my aunt used to draw the blinds, yet when I awoke they were always raised. Once I asked her if she came into my room while I slept to open the blinds. "No dear," she assured me, "I want you to get your rest."

It was our chef, Bogu, who named our ghost Marty. He was a funny, little round man with a handlebar moustache who we had known for years. We had met while working together in a restaurant in Miami. The first time we saw Bogu, he was wearing a cape, a little pointed hat, and was carrying a wand. He looked like Merlin. Bogu was interested in spells and magic and he did many magical things during the years that we knew him. As soon as he came to our restaurant in Sugar Loaf, he said, "Gail, this place is haunted. There's a strong presence here."

One night we left a pot of veal soup stock on the stove to simmer. Bruce shook me from sleep yelling, "Gail the place is on fire. We have to get out." The smoke was curling over our heads. We jumped up, grabbed Robin, and ran downstairs. As soon as we passed through the dining room, Bruce told us to relax — the building wasn't burning, but we still needed to go outside and get some air. He knew this, because he couldn't feel any heat. The stock had boiled away and the veal bones were burning on the bottom of the pot. It was the worst odor imaginable and we thought we'd never get rid of it. I was horrified because I feared we'd have to close the restaurant. We opened all the windows and doors, but the place continued to reek. Yet, Bogu consoled us by saying, "If you go away for a day, I can get rid of the odor."

So we took all our animals and left. Bogu went in and laid down circles of cards, lit candles, and preformed all sorts of magic things. Later, when we came back the smell was totally gone. We couldn't believe it, because we knew that this was a smell that permeated everything. Bogu said he used Marty's powers to get rid of the stench.

Bogu believed Marty spent most of his ghostly hours in Robin's bedroom. Robin was only five at the time, so I didn't mention it. However, it wasn't long before Robin began to tell us his own "Marty" stories. He saw him several times and used to complain that Marty kept him awake. The door to the attic stairs was in Robin's room and he complained that when he was in bed he'd hear a noise coming down the stairs. It sounded like a ball bouncing. Bogu told him to make friends with Marty by leaving him peace offerings of bread and water.

When asked about this years later, Robin said, "I used to leave them in places where my parents wouldn't find them, because I wanted to be sure it was Marty who drank the water and ate the bread. I would hide the offerings under my bed, or in the attic. They always disappeared. When I checked on them, it was as thrilling as finding the flag released on an ice fishing hole.

"I also saw Marty several times in the basement," Robin reported. "When I was a teenager I often worked late washing dishes. A couple of times I saw someone come down the stairs wearing black pants and a white shirt and assumed it was one of the waiters. Then I'd remember that I was alone and look up to see Marty walking toward the dumb-waiter at the end of the hall. Once I followed him, but he disappeared. Most of the people who have seen Marty have seen him treading down the basement stairs.

"Marty appears more frequently when there is any kind of construction going on in the restaurant. When we converted the front porch into a sunroom we happened to hire a new waitress. She knew nothing about our unearthly lodger. However, we knew she had been initiated by the end of her first night when she asked, 'Do you know you have a ghost?' Marty had just passed her on the stairs."

Gail smiles as she listens to Robin recount the story of the new waitress. Suddenly another incident comes back to her. It was the most bizarre manifestation that has surfaced since she and Bruce bought the Inn. It occurred in Robin's bedroom.

I walked in one day and saw a red symbol painted on his wall. I knew what it was, because I had just started to study Rune Stones. It was the symbol of spiritual initiation. Robin was still young and didn't know anything about the stones. I marched downstairs and demanded to know who painted the Rune symbol on my son's wall. The staff stared at me blankly. I'm sure they thought I was nuts.

Years later, I asked Robin to shut his eyes and reach in the bag to pull out a stone. The first stone a person draws is his special Rune forever. Robin drew the stone of spiritual initiation. He has fond memories of growing up with Marty. In fact, he now wears the symbol Marty gave him tattooed on his back.

Over the years, our waitresses, waiters and chefs have had a lot of fun with Marty, laughs Gail. Time after time, we've covered all the tables with tablecloths only to return with cutlery in hand to find all the cloths pooled on the floor. We're certain that whenever our manual dumb-waiter arrives empty, it's the work of his invisible hands. A few times the CD has stopped and we've heard a man's low voice singing through the speakers. We all chuckle and say, "Oh, that must be Marty." And whenever anything is missing, of course, he is the one who is blamed. Once in a while I've had a waitress who didn't want to be in the building at night by herself, but generally no one has thought of him as a negative or disruptive force. We mention him so much that everyone feels at ease. Marty may be a stow-away from another time, but he is as much a part of the Sugar Loaf Inn as the wide plank flooring and the creaky doors.

The Landmark Inn

Original water color by Gordon Richardson/ Courtesy of The Landmark Inn

Shortly after we bought the restaurant, I walked upstairs with our three-year-old Marissa to see how the renovations of our second floor living quarters were coming. Marissa toddled a room ahead. When I caught up to her, she pointed to the window and asked, "Who is that old lady?" "What old lady?" I asked. "There in the rocking chair," she demanded. No one was there — not even a rocking chair.

Rachel and Michael Di Martino bought the Landmark Inn in June of 1993. They are the fourth owners to use the 1774 farmhouse as a bar and restaurant. The house was originally built by Conrad Sly, who was one of the men who first settled in Warwick. He purchased the land from Robert Clark before the Revolutionary War. The only structure on the land at that time was a small Native American dwelling. The Sly family remained there for four generations.

Conrad Sly is also remembered as one of the blacksmiths who forged the iron links of the Great Chain that was strung across the Hudson River to prevent the British ships from sailing north from New York City in 1778.

The house began as a three room, log cabin which stood down the hill in the back of where the Landmark now stands. After the road was built, Conrad Sly had his oxen pull the house to its present position. It was there that he and his wife Anna Ward brought up their seven children and lived out their lives.

They passed their home down to their son, Colonel John Sly, and his wife Hannah Dekay, who in turn passed the house on to their son, Ross Winans Sly, and his wife Margaret E. Wilcox. Ross and Margaret had four children: John Winans, Norman Christie, Thomas Edward, and Hannah. None of their children ever married and it was Hannah who lived in the house the longest. She was born at home on November 19, 1866 and remained there until her death on March 16, 1950. At least that is when she was recorded to have left the house.

Shortly after we opened, Rachel continued, a customer reported the same sighting as our daughter Marissa. He told us, one night as he drove by the restaurant, he saw an old woman rocking in a chair in front of an upstairs window. He knew the building was vacant at the time, so he convinced himself he was overtired and had imagined it. Then a few weeks later, he saw the woman in the window again. This time his wife was sitting next to him and she saw the woman also.

Rachel and Michael wanted to know who this person was whose spirit appeared to their children and some of their customers. From time to time, old timers, past employees, and members of the Sly family who have dropped in have each filled in another piece of the puzzle. The majority of them suspect the Landmark ghost to be the spirit of Hannah Sly.

Orange County Historian Theodore W. Sly remembers visiting his second cousin Hannah at the Sly Homestead, with his brother Norman Thomas. "She was a reserved woman. I remember her refusing to have a toilet installed in the house as late as the 1940s. She'd say, 'I won't have one of those nasty things in my house.' Finally her maid Mary Hallock coaxed her to have an indoor bathroom shortly before she died." Norman, who is now the family genealogist, remembers Hannah always in a black dress with black high button shoes sitting in a rocking chair on the front porch. She wore her thin gray hair piled on top of her head in a tight knot and spoke in a soft voice.

When asked if the apparition could be Hannah, cousin Ruth Sly Masten replied, "No, Hannah was too mild mannered to linger where she shouldn't, the spirit is much more likely to be her mother Margaret. Margaret was an invalid and Hannah devoted most of her adult life to her care. When her mother felt well enough, Hannah would sit her in a rocking chair in front of an upstairs window so she could watch the traffic. She's much more likely to have an unhappy soul than Hannah."

Ruth remembers visiting Hannah and her brothers with her parents on Sunday afternoons. The family would gather in the dining room, which is now the tavern room, and listen to Hannah's oldest brother read from his diaries. Norman Sly now has these diaries in his library. Common entries were, "Mother was feeling smart today — she was able to sit up," and "Today we saw a car ride by." Margaret died of a general physical breakdown complicated by diabetes on June 18, 1919.

Hannah or Margaret have made her presence known in other ways, recounts Rachel. One night we were up late trying to fix the ice machine. My cousin, John, became frustrated and slipped into the dining room to take a breather. He discovered two candles lit on one of the tables. He blew them out. After he composed himself, he decided he had enough and went home. Mike and I went upstairs to bed shortly afterward. At around four in the morning I came down to the kitchen for a glass of water and discovered a candle burning on one of the tables. I blew it out and didn't think much of it.

The next day when John returned to help, he advised, "You need to tell the waitresses to be more careful. Last night two candles were left burning in the dining room." One of them was the same candle I discovered early that morning.

Landmark veteran Jim Reynard worked as the bartender and lived upstairs from 1973 to 1990, while Steve Kazmar owned the restaurant.

"I won't say I believe in ghosts, but after 18 years of strange happenings I can't say I'm a non-believer either," confessed Reynard. "Within the first six months, I noticed the torch lamps that stood on each side of the fireplace would be on and in the center of the room in the morning. Since they were the only lights that weren't on the main switch, they were always the last ones to be turned off. This used to happen two or three times a year. The first time I mentioned it to Steve, he said, 'A lot of strange things happen here, it's nothing to worry about.'"

Another common occurrence was the women's room toilet would flush by itself. We had plumbers look at it repeatedly, but they never found anything wrong.

When asked what was the weirdest disturbance he experienced, Reynard recalled that one Saturday night a waitress named Joan was carrying a relish tray back to the walk-in refrigerator. On the way into the fridge she glanced in the mirror, which hung to the left of the door. In the mirror she saw an old woman with a gray bun and a long black dress standing behind her. Joan put down the tray and turned to tell the woman that the dining room was closed, but she could still get a bite to eat in the barroom. When she didn't find the woman she searched the restaurant for her. She was nowhere to be found. Months later, Steve Kazmar was cleaning out the attic when he came across a photograph of Hannah Sly in a long black dress rocking on the front porch. He brought it downstairs to show his staff. Joan gasped, "That's the woman I saw in the mirror." That's when Hannah was first believed to be the spirit responsible for all of the strange happenings.

Carla Lichtenberger, who waitressed and bartended from 1981 to 1986, claims that every time she used the ladies' room, the door mysteriously swung open. After a while, she greeted the strange pleasantry with a thank you as naturally as she would if someone had held the door for her.

Another time Carla was sitting in the dining room reading before the restaurant opened when she heard a barrage of squeaky, creaking noises. The Landmark's dining room has a unique ceiling, which is made of antique doors. When Carla looked up, all the doorknobs were turning.

A few years after Joan sighted Hannah in the mirror, Carla was standing in front of the same mirror fixing her hair when she saw a small blond girl holding a teddy bear. She wore a white pinafore over a shin-length dress. When Carla turned around the girl was gone. No one has been able to surmise who this little girl was.

"Harmless things like these happened all the time," Reynard added. "There were only two incidents where someone could have gotten hurt. The first happened one morning when I was downstairs in the kitchen having coffee with Kitty Brandt. Kitty was a kind, old, Irish woman who was The Landmark's cook for over twenty years. She was very superstitious and was often spooked by the restaurant's ghostly goings-on. We were chatting, when we suddenly heard the most God-awful crash. It shook the whole building. We ran toward the sound in the adjoining barroom. The slate table had toppled over. The table was about six feet long, about three and a half feet wide and an inch and a quarter thick. It probably weighed 250 to 300 pounds. No table legs or floorboards were broken, so we couldn't explain what had prompted the crash. It required both Steve and me to pick it up. Poor Kitty fled to the parking lot clutching her Rosary. It took over twenty minutes to coax her back inside. Kitty was certain Hannah was furious about something.

"The second incident occurred one busy Saturday night around Christmas in 1983. I was off duty and relaxing at the bar when nine glasses flew off the shelves and crashed in different directions throughout the room. Oddly, it was only the front row of glasses that were hurled—the second and third never budged. I learned from customers that Hannah had been adamantly against liquor because her brother, Thomas Edward used to go into town on a 'toot' from time to time and not come back for days. Thomas shot himself in the head in an upstairs bedroom in 1908. Hannah was said to have blamed his demise on the drink. Incidentally, Thomas's suicide suggests that he is also a likely candidate for a haunting. No one has spotted him, yet. But you never know when he might appear.

The Di Martinos aren't sure whether they share their home and restaurant with Hannah or Margaret, or both, but they don't mind the presence they feel from time to time. They imagine that the Sly women are happy to have a family living in their home again. When asked what are their favorite pranks, Michael Di Martino replies, "The candles burning after I'm certain we've blown them out, and finding the two torch lamps lit and moved to the middle of the front parlor when we get up in the morning. They each happen around four or five times a year. We don't hear from Hannah and Margaret as often as the previous owners have, but every once in a while one of them still likes to remind us that she is here."

When thirteen-year-old Brianna Meinhardt entered the Landmark Inn's narrow, crooked bathroom and closed the door, it was empty.

There was a full-length mirror framed with Hollywood-style make-up lights to her right and a small sink with another mirror above it around the corner to her left. As she washed her hands, she saw that she was no longer alone. In the mirror she saw an elderly woman standing behind her. She wore a black dress and had thin, gray hair pulled back into a bun. She looked severe, yet, her warm eyes and gentle manner were reassuring. She asked Brianna how old she was, and how she liked school. Used to typical, old-lady questions, Brianna answered courteously and thought nothing of it. They continued to make small talk. Back at the table, Brianna's mother, Deni, started to feel uneasy. She went to look in on her daughter. "Who are you talking to?" she asked as she entered the room. "Her," Brianna answered as she turned to introduce her mother to her new acquaintance. The old woman had vanished. "She must have left as you came in," she insisted. "No one passed me," Deni smiled, "I think you just met the Landmark's ghost."

Hey You, Mr. Benson!

On a cold, wintry night in February of 1998, Maureen closed the bar by herself. It was two o'clock in the morning. Suddenly she heard the tinny sound of something hitting the floor upstairs in the restaurant and bounce across the tiles. She knew what it was. It was the holder for coffee machine filters. It had fallen the night before at the same time. And the night before that. "How could it rest securely on top of the spare coffee urn all day and then fall off hours after the restaurant has closed?" she wondered. "Was it blown off by the air from the heat vent? Perhaps that's it," Maureen told herself, knowing the vent was on the opposite side of the room from the beverage station.

The following night was Thursday. She tended bar on the busier nights with Renee. "Maurrreeen," a woman's voice whispered. She looked to see which customer wanted her attention. No one was ready for a refill. "Maurrreeen," the voice repeated. "Did you just call me?" She asked her co-worker. "No. Did you just tug the back of my shirt?" she answered. Stunned, the young women giggled nervously and resumed their work.

Another night when Renee was on by herself, she was cutting lemons to prepare the bar for the evening shift when she felt her hair sharply tugged. She turned to see who it was and saw that she was the only person downstairs. "Hey you!" a man's voice yelled abruptly. Again she turned to view an empty room. She walked upstairs to see if anyone had called her. Only two waitresses were left and they claimed they hadn't. She decided as long as she was upstairs she'd get more Corona for the bar out of the stock room. She picked up a case and then spotted the vodka she'd need to replace the near empty bottle downstairs. Carrying the case of beer, she gingerly stepped over a case of empties and reached for the vodka. She then placed the case down and laid on top a few more things that she thought she might need that evening. As she turned to leave, she steadied herself so she could step back over the case of empties when she saw the case had been slid out of her way to the other side of the room. Her heart thumped loudly. Someone had moved it, but who? The two waitresses hadn't moved from the table where they were winding down before going home.

The following night Renee mentioned these strange disturbances to Maureen. Maureen then confided more of her own experiences. The two women were convinced the village restaurant and tavern were haunted.

Since their realization, each of the bartenders and some of the waitresses have also heard her name whispered from time to time. It began subtly, only occurring when each person was alone. However, lately the voice has become more brazen. It now teases the waitresses even while they're serving a crowd. More and more of the employees have been summoned with a "Hey you!"

One night Maureen and Renee confided to a customer that they had frequently witnessed unseen forces while they worked. He was certain they were mistaken. Claiming he was attuned to that sort of thing, he told them that he had never sensed anything. The bartenders felt deflated. The idea of a ghost had become an exciting prospect.

A month later the same customer was chatting at the bar when he stopped mid-conversation. "I just saw your ghost," he exclaimed. "For an instant, I saw the vaporous outline of an elderly man standing in an overcoat, right there, under the TV." The tavern has a television set suspended from the ceiling on either side of the bar. The women felt validated. However, the owner of the restaurant still believed it was all nonsense.

Until one day when a woman with short, curly gray hair came in for lunch. A knowing smile crinkled out of the corners of her eyes. When Maureen asked what she could get her, the woman complimented her on the building's renovations. She confided that she had worked in the building forty years earlier. She followed with, "Do any odd things ever happen here?" Knowing immediately what she meant, Maureen gushed, "Yes!" and recounted the restaurant's repertoire of occurrences. "That's George Benson," said the older woman. "He owned this building for over fifty years. As soon as he passed away, he started turning the lights on and off and knocking things off the shelves. All of the employees continued to feel him looking over their shoulders the way he did when he was alive. He liked his business run smartly and he wasn't about to let it go just because he died. We used to joke how he must have gotten a kick out of letting us know he could still see us."

Then who is the woman who whispers our names?" Maureen bent closer. "Hmm," the woman thought for a moment, "I don't know. We only felt Mr. Benson." Ever since that afternoon, the man who haunts the village restaurant and pub has been referred to as Mr. Benson. And he continues to address them by name. If he is ignored he continues to shout, "Hey you!" The woman also continues to whisper the wait staffs' names, but they haven't identified her yet.

Ninety percent of the employees have heard their names called or the insistent, "Hey you!" Some people have even been startled by the movement of shadows crossing the room, which can only be seen reflected in the glass of the pictures hanging on the walls. For some reason Mr. Benson and a mysterious woman have chosen to remain. Perhaps they are simply unable to retire.

Every night the last person out the door says, "Goodnight, Mr. Benson."

The Curse of the Vail House

"It all began that very first day we began to remodel our new restaurant. People from the village dropped in throughout the afternoon. They welcomed us to Warwick, glance around nervously, and then tell us bits and pieces about the Vail family. They spoke in hushed-church voices as if they expected to be struck by lightning, especially when they spoke of Roy Vail, who was the last member of his family to have lived here while it was a residence. Then they always hesitated before asking the next question, 'Have you seen or heard any ghosts yet?'

"No, we lied, no ghosts here. But they were here all right," recalls Pina Muto. "My husband Silvio and I bought the Vail House Inn in 1993 and turned it into our restaurant The Italian Villa. We were immediately barraged with the sound of loud footfalls that stomped up and down the stairs, doors that opened and slammed, and our belongings being hurled and crashing into pieces. It was apparent someone didn't want us here.

"We didn't know about the house's ominous past except that the previous restaurant owner was met with financial ruin and abandoned it. We bought it as a foreclosure.

"As those early days and weeks passed Silvio and I tried not to focus on the local stories or our growing repertoire of disturbances, but we couldn't ignore what happened next. While working late, Silvio heard the front door click open and shut. When he went to see who it was, he was startled by the filmy figure of an old man clad in riding boots, a heavy overcoat, and hat. The specter ignored him and clomped purposefully up the staircase, down the hallway, into a bedroom and slammed the door.

"It was Roy Vail. We were certain. The vaporous vision fit the description we had heard over and over. A dreadful fear took possession of us. We were scared to death."

Roy had been described by some of the villagers as charming and by others as eccentric and cantankerous, even depressed at times. Some people adored him. In fact, some people loved him so much that they remain loyal to his memory even today and would prefer that I not tell this story, while others don't have a nice thing to say about him. One thing is certain — he made an impression.

Remembered as portly, he stood about five foot ten with receding gray hair and an aquiline nose. His mouth turned downward like the rim of a cup even when he smiled. He frequently wore a khaki-colored safari shirt, chinos, and riding boots or moccasins. He was a highly regarded member of The Warwick Valley Board of Education and a president of the Historical Society of the Town of Warwick. Out of his barn, he worked as a cabinetmaker, antique dealer, and gunsmith. Some of you may remember his barn, which was known as the Tai Chi Farm. It was recently torn down to make way for a housing development.

His gunsmith work was internationally recognized. He carried on the art of ornamenting and embellishing firearms. He carved stocks from different woods, inlaying them with ivory and precious metals in elaborate designs. He rebuilt the flintlock of George Washington's pistols, so they could be authentically displayed in West Point's museum. He also custom made a rifle for Dwight D. Eisenhower. Rumored to have the mercurial moods of an artist, Mr. Vail was not to be asked a lot of questions, such as when a customer's gun would be finished, lest the gun be handed back to its inquirer and he be told to leave.

He lived in this house all of his adult life. His parents, Harry and Cecelia Emily Utter Vail, purchased the farm in 1920, when Roy was 19 years old. They bought it from the Drew Family, who in turn had bought it sometime between 1850 and 1860. It was the Drew Family who added the second story and named the property Maple Glen Farm. Levi Ellis, a Revolutionary War Soldier, built the house circa 1792. It began as a three-room farmhouse and was enlarged by the Ellis Family in 1811. Roy inherited the house upon his father's death in 1949. There he and his wife, Edith, brought up their three children. After their children were grown and Edith lost her battle with cancer, Roy continued to live in his family's home until his suicide during the winter of 1979. He was 78 years old.

"How can we rid ourselves of these disturbances and the energy that has possessed Roy Vail to remain here?" Pina asked herself. "Something had to be done. Silvio and I called our priest.

"A few days later, he arrived with holy water and prayer book in hand. I rushed him in and took his coat. When I hung the coat in the closet a small piece of molding started to spin wildly. We froze. The priest peered over my shoulder. Without a word, he opened his prayer book and splashed Holy Water into the corners of the closet and front hall. The molding spun faster as though it were angered. Finally it stopped. My husband checked to see if the molding was loose. It was not. Our priest nervously remarked, "There is definitely something here and it doesn't like me." He completed the blessing and we hoped for the best.

"However, shortly afterward we got back pictures we had taken at different stages of our renovation and decorating projects. When we looked at the pictures, there they were. Smoky images of people we'd never seen stood in every shot. That was when we realized we didn't have a ghost. We had two or three. And the blessing hadn't thwarted them a bit.

"Who were the others? Customers continued to drift in with stories. Some were so embellished that to repeat them would further spread gossip. However, there is one story where truth has ceased to matter, because it has become a part of Warwick's lore. It is as much a part of the village's legends as the afternoon George Washington stopped at the Baird Tavern for a pint of grog. It is the story we hear the most often."

Roy sported a keen interest in Native American relics and history that began when he was a child living in the Amity section of town. During his boyhood he discovered a cave in the woods on his family's 56-acre farm. Inside, he found enough relics to establish that Native Americans used it as a place to camp or live. It is said that it was there that Roy exhumed the grave of a Leni Lenape Chief. Some people say he removed a copper bracelet from its remains. Others say he removed pottery. Whatever it was, this is where his trouble is believed to have started, because everyone knows that if you disturb an Indian Chief's burial ground you will be cursed forever.

Later in life, Roy's beloved sister Emily was discovered murdered in her home just a short walk away. Her homicide remains a mystery. Several myths about her murder still swirl through time, one of them is simply that by being Roy's sister she was also a victim of the Native American scourge.

Five years later, on December third, 1979, Roy was found dead at his kitchen table, having shot himself in the head that morning. One family member recalls his wife, Edith, predicting that if she were to die before him, he wouldn't live more than six months afterwards. It was six months since her death.

We also learned from a relative that shortly after Roy died, his grand-daughter came back to Warwick to visit her family. Since the Vail house was still in the family's possession, she and her family stayed there. That night she and her husband, along with their pet cat, slept in her grandparents' bed, while her children slept in the next room. Yowling in terror, the cat jolted the granddaughter from sleep. She sat up to catch the translucent figures of her grandparents standing by her bedside. They then floated into the children's room.

One of our waitresses claimed to have seen the Vail couple too. She was pulling out of the parking lot one night, when she glanced at the entryway of the restaurant and saw a dapper, old man in a tuxedo standing beside a woman in a green evening gown. They waved goodbye to her. She knew that only Silvio and the bartender were left in the building.

Another evening we had a party of twelve in our private room — the room that was once Roy's office. One of the guests informed me that he was the assistant chef when the restaurant was the Vail House Inn. He asked pointedly if we ever experienced anything strange. With my best poker face I asked what he meant. He explained that when he worked here two things happened frequently: one was the exhaust fans in the kitchen would suddenly stop, reverse direction and fill the kitchen with smoke; the other was that the lights often flickered on and off. Amazed, I confided that the same things were happening to us. Just then one of the waitresses motioned to me that she needed change. I gestured to her to please leave the checks on the workstation and I would take care of them in a moment.

When I excused myself the checks were no longer there. I assumed the waitress didn't want to keep her tables waiting and asked the bartender for change, until she rushed over looking flustered. "Where are the checks?" she asked anxiously, "My tables want to leave!"

We searched the whole restaurant. Unable to find them, we gave the customers their change without receipts and I returned to the former chef and his private party. They were bustling around the table while buttoning their coats. Their dinners were barely touched. They demanded their check. The chef was wound into an excitable panic. "The lights have flickered on and off since you left," he yelled. "Don't let Roy scare you," I urged, but they left anyway. They quickly paid and hurried out the door. Hours later, when I returned to the bar to make someone a drink, I came across the checks neatly placed by the beer cooler in plain sight.

Another time a distinguished, gray-haired gentleman with an elegant voice came in with friends for dinner. He seemed more than familiar with our building, so I asked what his connection was. He told me that he was the interior designer who orchestrated the transition from house to restaurant for the former owners.

He confided how his carpenters called him one evening to insist that they were quitting. They said they couldn't take the footsteps any longer. They claimed that when they worked upstairs they heard the locked, front door open and slam shut. Then heavy, booted footsteps thudded across the floors below. When they worked downstairs, the bedroom doors abruptly slammed upstairs and similar footfalls were heard.

After being coaxed to remain on the job, the carpenters demolished a small room to install a master bathroom upstairs. Under the old plasterboard, they discovered another wall. It was of "board and batten" style, which was commonly used at the turn of the century. Underneath there was another plaster wall. Deeply scored into the plaster was a symbol. The owner of the house believed it was a pentagram that symbolized black magic and insisted that the wall be removed. However, other people interpreted it as a spiritual symbol that may have even been a blessing. Nonetheless, the wall was torn down.

Within a few short years we had amassed a number of stories of our own, but I felt uncomfortable revealing them, because I didn't want to frighten our staff. Also my children were younger at the time and I had to make sure that they felt safe.

One wintry Saturday night around one o'clock in the morning, Silvio and I were in the restaurant with my brother-in-law and his wife and a few of our waitresses when the burglar alarm went off. It hadn't been set. It was deafening. We spread out and checked the building for intruders and found no one. Silvio raced downstairs and tried to turn off the alarm. Unable, he cut the wires in a panic. The alarm continued to scream. We called the central office and they swore that they hadn't been notified that our alarms had been tripped. We then called the police and asked why they hadn't come. They also had not been alerted. After fifteen minutes of torture, my husband said, "Let's get out of here. We'll deal with it tomorrow." With that, the alarm stopped. As we headed for the door the alarm went off again. Silvio hollered, "Mr. Vail, are you having fun? We're here to stay, so cut it out." The alarm silenced. The next day a new alarm was installed. There was never any explanation.

Even odder was an occurrence during the blizzard of 1996. A couple of our waiters spent the night upstairs. During the night they looked out the window to gauge the storm and saw the whole yard lit with an eerie light and the large oaks that lined our property were downed. They called us at home and asked what they should do. We asked if the trees had fallen onto the building. When they responded no, we told them not to worry, we'd have them cleared away the next morning. In the morning the trees were standing.

It took me until the following winter not to be afraid. One chilly, February night I locked the tavern door without having my car keys ready in my hand. Standing in the dark, I searched the bottom of my purse. I couldn't find them. Suddenly the parking lot lights turned on along with the porch lights on either side of the door. These lights are on a timer and always go off at 10:30 p.m., but I wasn't going to worry about them because I found my keys. I darted to my car and started the engine. As I turned on my headlights all the lights went off. "Oh my God," I groaned. That's when I knew Mr. Vail was looking out for me.

We accept Roy Vail and his wife Edith and whoever else is here, states Pina. Well not all of us. Felix, our red tabby cat is petrified to be left alone in the restaurant at night, preferring the outdoors even in subzero weather.

If our ghosts still linger because of a curse, it seems to have weakened or lived out its course. We know this because our things no longer careen across our rooms, the disturbances are gentler — quiet reminders that they are still with us. We have shared the Vail's home with them for ten years now. Yes, there is no doubt it is still their house. But we plan to stay and, apparently, so do they.

The curse of the Vail House goes on. Recently the owners acquired a picture of the man who haunts their restaurant, Roy Vail. They showed it to a few people and placed it aside until they had time to have it matted and framed, so it could be displayed in the front hall with the other historic pictures. Within minutes it vanished. Was this caper the work of Roy Vail, himself?

FOUR
FRIGHTENING ACCOUNTS BROUGHT TO WARWICK

The Girl on the Swing

Christine Cole Pen & Ink

The Ouija Board

Nathan was an Art major at New Paltz University. One evening in 1968, his roommate John and a few of their friends persuaded him to bring out his Ouija Board. They had knocked back a few beers and were looking for some laughs. They asked typical young people's questions such as, "Who will I marry?", "Will I graduate?", that sort of thing. As expected, the pointer drifted to the "Yes" and "No" printed at the top of the board. Nothing unusual happened, at least not then. The evening waned and the young men retired to their dorm rooms. After everyone left, John self-consciously asked Nathan if they could ask the board to contact his girlfriend, Carol.

John had been in a horrific car accident earlier in the school year where he suffered traumatic injuries and Carol was killed. The accident occurred as the couple was driving back to school from a carnival. They partook in the usual games, which included a fortuneteller who read their Tarot cards. The gypsy laid out the cards in a Celtic Cross Spread, looked into Carol's eyes and then without speaking scooped the cards back into a pile. "Is something wrong?" Carol asked. "You have no future," the woman replied. Tragically, her prediction came true within a few short hours.

Nathan was tired, but he could see how important this was to his roommate. Since the accident, John had become withdrawn and was wound into a desperate pursuit for a sign from his girlfriend's spirit. If it would bring him some consolation, maybe consulting the board was worth a try.

Soon after they placed their fingertips on the pointer, John started to act strange. He stared past Nathan and spoke in a trance-like voice. Nathan feared John was having a break down and needed medical care. He kept repeating, "There's this guy who's come out of the board who wants me to go with him." Certain that only a wall was behind him, Nathan pressed his back firmly against the wall as his friend faced him. He then flipped on his tape recorder. John continued to quiver, "He's here and he's saying, 'Come with me.' He's going to take me to Carol." "What does he look like?" Nathan asked. "He looks mean. He's old with white hair and is wearing a dark suit."

Nathan pleaded, "Don't go with him, John. Stay with me. He's not going to take you to Carol."

Thwap! Someone hit Nathan sharply on the back of the head. He spun around and upon seeing the man described, bolted up, flipped over the table, and ran from the room with John at his heels. The two got into Nathan's car and headed for the next town where they spent the rest of the night in a hotel.

Shaken, Nathan was convinced whoever they contacted was evil and his friend was in danger if they continued to use the board. The following day, he smashed the pointer and vowed never to use a Ouija Board again.

The Girl in the White Dress

Laura flipped through the Rockland County paper. She and her husband Dean had lived in Warwick for over five years, but she still subscribed to The Journal News to keep up with what was happening in her hometown of Nyack, New York. As she turned to the second section, her eyes went immediately to a picture of an old house. It was her old house.

Pictures of the exterior and interior sprawled across two pages. The house was an 1860 Victorian shingle-style farmhouse. It had a large wrap-around porch, which was half enclosed with mullioned glass. The new owners proudly displayed their recently restored carriage house and the recaptured country elegance of their home. But their renovations were not the reason this couple's story appeared in the paper. Their story was spiced with something extraordinary — the specter of a little girl.

Laura never saw the ghost of a little girl, but she knew all about her and read on as her heart pounded in her ears. The current owners relayed, "A few years ago, a friend who was visiting for the first time saw a little girl in a white dress on the swing out by the barn. The girl told her she lived in the room with the rounded mirror and that she spent her time with the person who twirls her hair." Odd little thing, the visitor thought and searched out her hosts.

The homeowners knew nothing about a little girl, but they showed their guest that they did, indeed, have an upstairs bedroom with a built-in vanity above which stood an arched mirror. And the lady of the house confessed that she did have a nervous habit of twirling her hair around her finger.

Laura also knew about the room with the arched mirror. It had been her bedroom from the year she turned ten until she went away to college. And she remembered when her father first hung the swing by the barn for her.

The couple in the article admitted that they weren't shocked by their guest's sighting, because they often turned off appliances that mysteriously switched on and heard doors slam in vacant areas of the house.

As a child, Laura didn't like the house. It seemed to ramble endlessly into an eerie past that no one mentioned, but could be felt.

Rather than go inside when the rest of the family was out, she'd climb the magnolia in the front yard and wait for their return. Once, she fell asleep in the tree and had to be carried into the house and put to bed. She knew if she went inside, the stereo would turn on by itself, and their collie would bark incessantly at some aberration only he could sense in the dining room. Although their collie was a much-loved pet, he had come unexpectedly as part of the estate. His owner had died from a heart attack in the dining room.

Laura told her parents repeatedly that their house was haunted, but they placated her by saying she could leave her light on when she went to bed.

When Laura was twelve her best friend, Ann, who lived next door, was given a Ouija board for her birthday. Ann also believed she had a ghost. Since her parents didn't believe her either, the girls had only each other to confide in about the spirits who shared their homes. Their first question to the oracle was, "Do we have ghosts in our homes?" The pointer sped to the word "Yes" at the top left side of the board. Spooked and intrigued, the girls asked their spirits their names. They were told odd names that didn't make sense. Laura's spirit said her name was "Satanas." Too innocent to notice its similarity to the word Satan, Laura didn't become frightened until she made the connection years later. The girls decided that when a person dies, she is given an unearthly, spiritual name.

Laura asked Satanas how she died. The pointer slowly spelled P-O-L-I-O. She wrote down the word and asked her mother what it meant. Her mother explained that it was a crippling and often deadly virus that afflicted many children before the 1960s. Amazed at the information they gathered, Laura and Ann became addicted to the Ouija Board and actively consulted it over the next two years. However, Laura feared that there might be an evil force that lurked beneath it and would only query the board in Ann's house. Ann was brave and confident and her home felt safer.

After months of closed-curtained communication, the girls felt sure enough of their findings to tell their classmates of their adventures into the occult. The skeptical ones demanded proof. When it came time to unveil the gateway to their secrets, the tiny tack was missing from the pointer. Without the tack, the pointer was useless. The disbelievers left satisfied that the girls were fakes. Laura and Ann mysteriously came across the tack as soon as they were alone again.

Although Laura learned all about her otherworldly roommate, she never felt at ease. To this day she wishes she could wave these memories off as a young girl's imagination. However, a recent newspaper article about her childhood home has made her early encounters with the supernatural even more unsettling.

The Ghost Who Moved From Chester to Warwick

In 1969 Moira moved her bridal trousseau, art supplies, and the few things she'd brought from Ireland into the towering Victorian Queen Anne home that had belonged to her husband Brahm's family for 75 years. She was 22 years old and the house with its 12-foot-high ceilings and dark, oak paneled walls overwhelmed her with its eerie darkness.

Built in 1856 by William Rysdyk, owner of the famous stallion, trotter Hambletonian, the elegant house announced the luck that catapulted Rysdyk from a farmhand to the wealthy owner of the most famous Standardbred horse in the world. It was three stories tall with an imposing front gable and a full-width porch. Decorative brackets accentuated the overhangs; the left side of the house was graced with a porte-cochere while the right had another small entry, and a mullioned glass porch that led into the kitchen.

Moira recalls an evening four years after she moved into the house. By this time she and Brahm had two boys and she remembers feeling exceptionally tired. It was a Thursday and she and Brahm were reading in the library the way they often did before they turned in. Unable to stay awake, she decided to go to bed early. Brahm assured he'd join her as soon as he finished his chapter. Moira got ready for bed as usual, checked on their two little boys, and settled into bed. Without warning, she heard a violent crash on the floor above her. Then she heard a long dragging sound that vibrated the ceiling. A pause. Another screeching drag of what sounded like a large piece of furniture. Another pause, as though someone was trying to rally his strength before the next tug. The drags and pauses continued. Moira lay dead still and lined up her options. She could be brave and go up to the third floor and surprise the intruder by bolting into the room, but then what would she do? Or she could creep down to the library and coax Brahm to investigate. Or she could stay in bed and hope that whoever it was would go away. Right then, the sound passed through the wall that partitioned the two rooms above her. Realizing that the sound was not of this world, she froze with fear and had no choice except her third plan. She scooted down and covered her head with the sheets and blankets. Her heart raced like a riptide. She could barely breathe. Time passed.

Brahm finally came to bed. Moira blurted out what had been the most frightening moments of her life. Brahm looked at her strangely. He had lived in this house practically all his life and he had never experienced anything odd. "Didn't you hear that huge crash?" she asked astonished. "No Moirey. I'm tired, let's go to sleep." Moira knew she would never sleep unless she knew for certain that nothing was upstairs. She urged her husband to look. He acquiesced and returned saying, "The third floor looks the same as it always does. Now go to sleep."

Two evenings later Moira and Brahm hired their neighbors' daughter Kelly to babysit for their boys while they went out for a few hours. When they returned, they found her sitting at the kitchen table by the back door. She was as white as a ghost. She quivered, "I was sitting in the library when I heard this loud noise. Then I heard something drag across the floor. I thought the boys had gotten out of bed and were shoving their furniture around. When I raced into their room and found them in their beds, I suspected they were pretending to be asleep. So I scolded, 'I know you're awake,' but they didn't move and I realized from their soft, steady breathing that they weren't fooling. As I walked into the hallway I heard the noise again. It was coming from the third floor. I fled downstairs and have been waiting for you to come home ever since."

Moira could see how frightened the young girl was and tried to comfort her by saying in a calm voice, "It was probably just squirrels up in the attic." She struggled to remain aloof and practical, the way Brahm had two evenings before. "Let me walk you home, Love."

As they crossed the lawn she pressed for more information, "Now tell me everything that happened again, so we can try to make sense of this." Kelly repeated that there was this awful crash and then it sounded as if something was dragged across the floor. "It would drag and then stop, drag and then stop. It went on for what seemed like forever." Moira was frightened. "It was exactly what she heard last Thursday," she thought. "What could it be?"

She hurried home. Brahm would have to take her seriously now. How could two people hear the same thing and nothing be there? Her husband listened patiently as she recounted the same story she had told a couple of nights ago. "I already checked the third floor and there is nothing up there," he said matter-of-factly. She protested, but he responded with an expression he heard her use often, "I think you've gone a bit daft." She laughed. There wasn't any point in discussing it further, but she continued to wonder what had happened on the third floor that continued to repeat itself and echo down through history. Could it be William Rysdyk's spirit trying to come to terms with some wrongdoing or was it one of Brahm's ancestors reluctant to leave their elegant home?

A few months later she was about to step into the shower when she heard her mother-in-law's voice calling after her up the stairs. "Moirey," the singsong voice called. "Moirey, Moirey." "I'm just getting into the shower Mum. I'll be down in a few minutes." When she threw on her robe and went downstairs, the house stood empty. "I wonder why she couldn't wait?" she thought. Later that afternoon when her mother-in-law phoned, she asked what her hurry was earlier. "What? I haven't been out of the house all day," she responded. Moira puzzled. The voice had unmistakably been Brahm's mother's.

She decided not to mention it to her husband, but to tell her own mother instead. She and her sisters had always kidded their mother about being a witch. While they were growing up, their mother often shocked them with her keen intuition and was known to see spirits from time to time. She claimed that it was a gift from having been born the seventh child of a seventh child.

After hearing about the goings-on in Chester, New York, her mother confided, "I didn't want to scare you, but when I visited last summer I saw an apparition of two soldiers from time to time in several areas of the house. They were wearing gray uniforms and had swords hanging at their sides." "If she mentioned this one, Brahm would surely think her whole family was crazy," thought Moira.

A couple of months later, her brother, Brendan, and his girlfriend, Angie, visited from Ireland. Brendan came downstairs in the morning and said Angie was too upset to stay another night. She heard a woman's voice taunt her all night by calling her name. Moira and Brahm looked at one another. "That's ridiculous," Brahm chuckled, "Who would be calling Angie? She doesn't know anyone in the States except us and your sister Kathleen." Moira thought back to the morning that she heard her mother-in-law's voice as she stepped in the shower. "Maybe she'll feel safer if she sleeps in a different room." Again, Angie was haunted by the phantom caller. She and Brendan cut their visit short and went on to visit Kathleen. Brahm shook his head and teased, "You Irish women sure are a superstitious lot."

Odd things continued to happen. Every once in a while as she walked out of the boys' room Moira caught sight of a person's shadow shimmering across the wall of the staircase as if someone had just crested the stairs and passed her in the hall. And whenever she painted in her studio, she saw shadows darting out of the corners of her eyes. She would turn and catch a wisp of something and then it would be gone.

Although Moira had learned to love the old house with its romantic nooks and niches, it had become a struggle to keep up and she often wished for a larger yard for their boys that wasn't on a main street in the village.

In 1979 she and Brahm built a house in the nearby town of Warwick. They were scarcely there a week when Moira was awakened early in the morning. She recalls looking at the alarm clock on the nightstand and reading 5:13. She also remembers that it was yet another Thursday. As she changed her position, she came face to face with a man in a gray uniform and a shiny black hat suspended over her. "Oh my God," she gulped. The apparition didn't seem to notice her. It only appeared from the waist up and hung in the air looking down at her husband lying beside her. "Who the hell are you?" she demanded. The apparition never changed its gaze and hovered over the bed for another ten minutes. Moira stared amazed. Seeing his chest heavily decorated with medals and ribbons, she thought he must have been an officer. She also noticed she could see her dresser and the picture on the wall as she looked through him. After a while he slowly tilted his head toward the window and seemed to be sucked through the screen. She then rushed to the window expecting to see him floating in the dawn sky. But he had vanished.

"Brahm, wake up. You'll never believe what just happened." This time he sat up and listened with rapt attention. "Now tell me everything about him." For the first time he didn't doubt her. That afternoon he brought out a box of old family photographs. He showed her a picture of his grandfather in a German army uniform taken in 1914. "Is this the man you saw?" he asked, as he held the picture of the man he was named after. Moira looked at the dark-haired gentleman who proudly displayed his medals in a gray uniform. "It is!" she said even more amazed.

Brahm's grandfather never lived in or even saw the house in Chester. Yet, he seems to be one of the soldiers sighted by her mother in their Chester home and again by Moira, herself, in their Warwick home. Perhaps from time to time he travels from beyond the grave to check on his namesake. And what is it about Thursdays? No one knows.

Death Valley Ranch

It was one of the last nights of the summer we were fourteen. Sharon was back from her family's traditional three-week trek across the country and we were ready for a beach night. Summers were what Greenwood Lake was all about, especially if you were a kid. Except for church and eating meals with our families, we pretty much lived on the beach. Most of the summer kids had gone back to the city and we looked forward to being with just our neighborhood gang again. It wasn't long before Diana, Karen, Brian, Bruce, and Nicky joined us. Our group was now complete.

A breeze picked up off the lake. It was a perfect night for a campfire. Even better it was a perfect night for a ghost story. We took our places on the moonlit sand. "Who wants to go first?" asked Diana as the trees blew dappled shadows across our faces. Sharon sat wide-eyed and frozen. We waited for her to speak. "Sharon, you must have a story from your trip?" Diana prodded. "I do," she hedged, "but I promised my parents I'd never tell anyone." "Oh c'mon," we pleaded. Sitting crosslegged in her plaid short ensemble and her chestnut bob Sharon looked panicked. "You don't have to tell us if you don't want to," I said, coming to her rescue. "Yes she does," Diana announced, "I can tell it's a good one. Ple-e-ease, Sharon." "All right," Sharon acquiesced looking slightly relieved, "but you have to promise never to tell anyone. My dad says he'll lose his job if this story gets around. And that people will think we're crazy. But I swear this really happened."

Sharon began, "We left Ridgecrest, California, early that morning, so it wouldn't be searing hot when we reached Scotty's Castle on our way across Death Valley. A park ranger advised us not to take the desert lightly, to pack plenty of water, and never to get out of the car. From the sides of the highway signs warned, "Last Stop for Gas in Fifteen Miles," "Last Chance to Fill Up," "Fill Up Now, or Else!"

After two hours my brothers, sister, and I were bored with the desert. Even with air conditioning it was hot and Mom had let the goodies in the picnic basket run low. To make matters worse, she replaced our Crosby, Stills and Nash eight-track with her Neil Diamond. We became unbearable, so Dad gave up the idea of reaching Las Vegas by nightfall and stopped at The Furnace Creek Museum to break up the day. Mom and Nana made sure my father knew this was not going to be a camping night. It was a motel night — an air-conditioned motel.

When we got into the car we still had three more hours of desert driving before we hit Nevada and my little sister Linda had already started to whine. We drove and drove and drove. As it grew dark all of us complained of hunger. Dad promised that he would stop for dinner at the next place we came upon.

Lulled by the vibration of my head against the window, I saw my first shooting star. I wished that a restaurant would appear on the side of the road in the next five minutes. Then dozens of shooting stars shot across the sky. We counted twenty-three. Soon we noticed the blue-white glow of neon in the distance and hoped for hamburgers and bathrooms. Mom prayed for the coolness of line-dried sheets. Our prayers and wishes were answered, or so we thought. There it was "Death Valley Ranch." It had a restaurant, motel, and vacancies! A large ram's head flashed from either side of the sign.

Linda and I ran ahead into the restaurant. It was icy cold inside, which at first felt refreshing. When we piled into the bathroom an old lady with long, stringy gray hair turned from the sink. She looked us up and down with a slight smile revealing rotted teeth. Her eyes were a faded, milky blue. "Where ya from?" she asked. "New York," I yelled as I rushed passed her into a vacant stall. Her voice crackled into a "Wicked Witch of the West" laugh.

When we joined our family in the chilly, vinyl booth, my mother went to the car to get everyone sweaters. I didn't care about the temperature, now that I had peed all I felt were hunger pangs. While we waited we all looked around the room. Every painting displayed the same odd symbol. "Dad, what do the five pointed stars in the circles mean?" I asked. "I don't know, maybe it's an astrology sign," he answered. Mom came back and handed out sweaters. She scanned the room and asked, "Look, isn't that a sign for black magic?" "It's an astrology sign," Linda assured her sounding like an authority.

"It's not any astrology sign that I know of," she answered. We all sat quietly, deep in our own thoughts. "It's colder than a meat locker in here," Mom complained as she continued to look warily around the restaurant. Nana shifted uncomfortably.

Just then the waitress hobbled toward our table to take our order. She had a pronounced limp. She sort of rolled forward on one white, sandal, while the other slammed the floor with the stiffness of a wooden leg. Linda was the only one who had the guts to ask why she walked funny. "Shush," Dad scolded, "I'll tell you later."

"What'll it be?" she snapped. We all looked into her pasty face framed by years of over-bleached hair. Holding the order pad and pen, her hands sported nails that were painted black and filed into points like claws. We each gave our order in turn. The round was broken by silence. We all looked to Mom to order. We followed her eyes to the woman's necklace. Its charm was the same symbol that was in each of the paintings except that it had a skull in the middle with ram's horns. "I'm sorry," my mother said politely, "But suddenly I feel ill. We have to leave." "But Mom," my brothers groaned. "Do as your mother says and go to the car," my father insisted with an abruptness that was scarier than the necklace. We bolted toward the parking lot. I was petrified someone would try to stop us. We walked as fast as we could, hoping not to draw attention to ourselves. Soon I felt someone swoop up behind me. I could feel their cold breathe down my neck. My body went prickly all over and I started having tunnel vision. Voices sounded far away. Above my pounding heart I heard the waitress tease, "What's the matter, the desert take all the fun out of ya?" I didn't dare look back.

Once in the car Mom doubled over out the car door and threw up. "Don't worry," my father comforted, "I'll have us out of here in a minute." "Please," was the only word she could muster. When dad turned the key the car seemed to groan, nooo, nooo, nooo. It didn't start. "Damn it!" he yelled punching the steering wheel. Now I felt like I was going to throw up. He tried again. The car complained again, then started to sputter. Dad revved the engine a few times, threw it into reverse, and floored it out of the parking lot. We were all still hungry, but we didn't dare raise a fuss. Until Linda braved, "Dad what was wrong with that lady's leg?" "She had a club foot, which means she didn't have spaces between her toes." "Her and Satan himself," murmured Nana.

After we crossed into Nevada, we stopped at the first gas station. As the attendant filled our tank, Dad asked, 'Could you tell us where the closest place is to get a bite? Any place except that ranch twenty-five miles west of here.' 'Ranch twenty-five miles west of here?' the man repeated. 'Yea,' my father answered, 'The Death Valley Ranch.' The man's eyes grew round. Then he grinned, 'You're kiddin' me, right?' 'No, we were just there, but my wife got a little spooked so we left.' The man swallowed hard. 'That place burned down in the 1930s. Supposedly, it was a meeting place for devil worshippers or some-thing.' My father and the attendant stared at each other with their jaws unhinged until my father said, 'Thank you for your help,' and we left."

Sharon's voice began to quiver and she again begged us never to tell anyone. I could tell she already regretted her faith in us. Her father was right, it was too fantastic a story to keep to ourselves. I'm certain we all told our parents the minute we walked in the door. At least I know I did.

That night we walked each other home in silence, starring straight ahead. Sharon and I lived the farthest from the beach, so I walked her home last before heading for my house next door. As she climbed her front steps I said, "That was the scariest ghost story I've ever heard." Sharon nodded still looking shaken and shut the door.

FIVE
SUPERNATURAL MOMENTS

Crows

Christine Cole Pen & Ink

1) Applewood Orchards ~ Everyone in the Warwick Valley knows David and Susie Hull of Applewood Orchards, but hardly anyone knows what takes place in their 300-year-old stone home after dark. Paintings aren't just mysteriously removed from their walls, they materialize in different rooms.

Incidentally, according to David Hull's brother, Richard W. Hull in his book "History of Warwick, New York," the stone home is the oldest house not only in the Warwick Valley, but in all of Orange County, New York. It was built by Dr. Samuel G. Staats who was, among many things, a land speculator. Etched into a stone by the front entrance are his initials along with the year the house was erected, "S.G.S. 1700." Perhaps Dr. Staats has a penchant for re-decorating.

2) The 1770 Lazear Tavern ~ This was once the residence of Emily Vail whom you heard mentioned in "The Curse of the Vail House Inn." On August 4, 1974, Ms. Vail was found brutally murdered in her real estate office in the rear section of the first floor. Her homicide still remains inconclusive. After her estate was settled, Susie Stage bought the quaint colonial despite its blood curdling history. One afternoon I asked Susie if she ever was visited by Ms. Vail's ghost during her years there. She quickly answered, "No." But later that evening she asked her son Patrick if he ever saw anything. "Oh yeah," he recalled, "every once in a while I'd wake up to find a gray-haired lady at my bedside, smiling at me."

3) The 1760 McFarland Farm ~ In 1981 Abigail McFarland Opper brought four friends home from college. While she cooked dinner, she left them to entertain themselves in the living room. "Abbey!" a man's

voice loudly summoned. Thinking it was one of her friends, Abigail calmly answered in a singsong voice, "Be there in a minute." "Abbey!" the voice boomed fiercely. "Now you just hold your horses!" she snapped. She then rushed into the living room to demand what was so urgent. Staring at her blankly, her friends swore that they hadn't called her. Instantly, Abbey knew who had roared her name so rudely. Nonplussed, she flipped her long red hair and marched back to her cooking. Once back in the kitchen she announced, "James, I am not your wife."

This voice from beyond was no surprise to Abbey, because she was brought up surrounded in ancestral history. Her parents, Donald and Mary Neal McFarland, have detailed records of their family's genealogy. She is a descendant of Daniel Burt, who built what is now the oldest house in the village of Warwick. This early home is now a museum known as "The Shingle House." In 1760, Daniel moved his family to the farm just outside the village that now belongs to the McFarlands. There, he and his wife, Hannah Benedict, brought up their ten children. They handed the house down to their youngest son, James, who married Abigail Coe in 1783. James and Abigail also lived out their lives in the house before leaving it to their son James and his wife, Mary Gilette Harding, who in turn bequeathed the house to James's sister, Abigail Burt Martine. The farm has remained in the family for over 240 years. Three Abigails have padded through the farmhouse's rambling halls. Named after Abigail Burt Martine, Abigail McFarland Opper was the third.

4) A Mayor's Story ~ When Michael Newhard first bought the 1840 Adam-style, Colonial he now lives in with his wife Judy Pedersen and their son Henry, he worked on its restoration many nights until

dawn. A presence often joined him on the staircase. Michael believed the spirit belonged to former owner John McElroy, who crossed over to inspect the reconstruction. McElroy's parents James and Martha built the house when they were first married. John lived there his entire life and worked as a schoolmaster in Warwick. Whoever the specter was, he must have been satisfied, because he hasn't been felt since Michael revived their home from its grim, crumbling state to the light, elegant showplace it is today. Just as uncanny was Michael's childhood intuition that he would grow up to live in this house. Was it intuition or was it the lure of the spectral schoolmaster who knew who to choose to save his home?

5) Warwick's Historian ~ Every town has a person informally known as the village historian — in Warwick that person is Bill Raynor. I spent many afternoons in Raynor's Market & Groceries picking Bill's brain for details to flesh out the stories in this collection. One afternoon he smiled slyly with a mischievous, blue-eyed-twinkle and admitted that he had a story of his own.

In 1906 his grandparents, Lucy and Fred Raynor, lived out on Welling Avenue. While there, Lucy had a baby and her mother, Evelyn McWhorter Smith, came to help out. Dismally, she wasn't able to help for long. One evening Grandma Smith tripped while walking down the back staircase to the kitchen and fell to her death. Or at least that is what everyone thought.

Years later Smith's granddaughter, Evelyn, visited her father, Fred Raynor, in St. Petersburg, Florida. Incidentally, Evelyn was the very baby whom her grandmother was taking care of when she died. During her stay, they attended a tent show. Appearing that night was a psychic. Fred and Evelyn took their seats in the audience. A gypsy with a bandana wrapped around her head sat facing them. Her eyes were half closed and she had a slight sneer on her lips. Her face twitched as she spoke. Evelyn remembers the psychic's voice changed with each person she addressed. Then she asked, "Is Evelyn or Eva here tonight?" Fred and his daughter traded meaningful glances. The psychic repeated the question two more times. Evelyn was too scared to raise her hand. Not only did she fear she was the Evelyn being summoned, she suspected that the Eva being sought was her aunt. Aunt Eva was her mother Lucy's sister and Grandma Evelyn Smith was their mother. "Why don't you speak to her," the psychic barked, "She's standing right behind ya!" Evelyn and her father shook with terror. "It's me, your grandmother," the psychic growled, "I just want you to know that I was still alive!" Coincidence? Or was the gypsy channeling poor Evelyn McWhorter Smith, who until that moment was believed to have died instantly from her dreadful accident on the stairs.

6) The Farm ~ For twenty years, the spirit of Louise Mayewski has joined Barbara and John White every night in their bedroom to watch the eleven o'clock news. Before John was convinced of this, Barbara propped a chair against their bedroom door to prove what she already knew. Sure enough at eleven o'clock the chair toppled over and the door creaked open. The Whites are certain that Mrs. Mayewski is the ghost who joins them at eleven. It was Barbara who saved her farm from being subdivided and developed. Barbara works as a realtor and showed the farm to a couple who wanted to buy it.

When they mentioned knocking the 200-year-old farmhouse and its barns down, she convinced the couple to abandon their plans. They, in turn, convinced her to buy the property. They even promised to hold her mortgage if she found them another farm to buy. Mrs. Mayewski is forever grateful and now and then can still be heard giggling in the attic.

7) In 1978 Dean and Debbie Krzymowski moved into their elegant 1859 Victorian Second Empire in Florida, New York. While Debbie was cleaning the room that was once used by Dr. Jesse D. Mars for his practice, she was startled by the dark shadow of a bird as it swooped down at her. She ducked and covered her face. After its wings fluttered past her arms, she peaked to see where it landed. No bird in sight. A month later the same phenomenon recurred. Was the banshee bird the morphed spirit of Dr. Mars? "…Open here I flung the shutter, when, with many a flirt and flutter, In there stepped a stately Raven of the saintly days of yore.… Tell me what thy lordly name is on the Night's Plutonian shore! Quoth the Raven, 'Nevermore.'" E. A. P.

8) The stately yellow Greek Revival on Colonial Avenue in Warwick was at one time owned by a family who felt so much supernatural activity that they hired a psychic to come and hold a séance. Upon entering the house, the psychic refused to stay. She claimed, "There are so many spirits in Warwick that a séance will only stir them up. And who knows what will happen!"

9) Greck's Maplewood Inn ~ Doris Greck Martin and her daughter, Sally Joe Warnock of Greenwood Lake claim every

time they took a vacation from their family restaurant, a plumbing mishap occurred that involved water damage. They attribute this strange coincidence to a warning that was often made by Doris's dad, "Never let this place be tended by anyone other than a Greek!"

10) de Roberts' Hair & Skin Establishment ~ Ruth and Joe de Roberts have a female wraith in the northwest corner of their building. She has tugged people's shirts, flung their extensive tin collection across the shop, rearranged their knick-knacks, and from time to time has flipped their lights and television on and off. These are all typical ghost shenanigans. But listen to this, the other morning she placed two logs in the shop's large, open-hearth fireplace and had a lovely fire burning for Joe and Ruth when they came downstairs. Until now, this had been Joe's morning ritual. Thinking, of course, that Ruth started the fire he turned and thanked her. She swore she hadn't. Who then?

The de Roberts's 1780 Salt Box has three tunnels underneath which were used during the years of the "Underground Railroad." One of their walk-in fireplaces was actually used to hide slaves. Is their spirit a slave who liked what she saw and stayed, or is she a former owner of the building? We may never know.

11) The 1819 Bellvale Farm ~ During the 1970s, Lenny and Louise Silver rented an apartment in the farmhouse of one of Warwick's most bucolic farms. They mentioned to landlords Al and Judy Buckbee that they often heard the sound of children's voices before they fell asleep. The Buckbees relayed that 100 years earlier

that part of the house was used as a schoolhouse. Although they have never heard anything unexplainable, other tenants have also reported strange happenings.

12) The Benedict House ~ Built by Captain Benedict in 1779, the sturdy stone Dutch Colonial that stands across from the Good Shepherd Lutheran Church is said to harbor a ghost. One of its previous owners, the late Reverend Joseph Sefl used the home's ghostly energy for a positive means. He held séances where he sought to tap into the ghost's other-worldliness to heal the sick. Reverend Sefl is remembered for his Spiritual Healing Services.

13) The 1739 Smith-Borroughs House ~ Incidentally, the historic Dutch Colonial Stone House farther north on Kings Highway is rumored to have a ghost-in-residence. Since it's currently vacant, we will have to wait for its next owner to tell us if it's true.

14) When Angela and Peter built their center hall Colonial in 1988 in Sugar Loaf, the last thing they ever imagined was having a ghost. As far as they know, the property was only previously used as a cow pasture. But mysterious things can happen in cow pastures. The day they moved in something moved in with them. Phantom footsteps were heard treading across their upstairs bedroom when they were downstairs and downstairs when they were upstairs. They even heard someone's quick nervous steps in the attic while they were in bed. This happened sporadically for three years. One night Angela was jerked out of sleep by someone yanking her big toe. She bolted upright and caught sight of the vaporous figure of a woman standing at the end of her bed. Yet another time she was

awakened by the terrifying sound of a woman screaming, "No!" as if she were being beaten in the basement. Whoever this woman was, she seems to have communicated all she needed, because she hasn't been heard from since.

15) Wickham Village ~ In 1986 when Debbie and Eddy Ewald moved into a ranch-style home with their one-year-old son Alex, Debbie felt such a strong presence that she found herself always turning around to see who stood behind her. One afternoon when Alex was three, Debbie remembers him looking up from his toys and asking, "Who said that?" "Who said what?" she asked. Alex lowered his chin to his chest and said in his deepest voice, "Hellooo Alex." "I don't know," Debbie answered, "I don't see anyone here except you and me." "Mommy, I heard him again!" "What did he say this time?" asked Debbie. Again Alex mimicked, "Hellooo Alex." Later Debbie learned from a neighbor that her home's former owner was an elderly man named Mr. Smith. She described him as a pleasant person who loved children. Because he had trouble walking, she used to help out by doing his grocery shopping. One morning when she brought the groceries in the back door, she discovered Mr. Smith dead in his recliner in the living room. As soon as Debbie learned who their spirit was, she and Alex never heard from him again. Did Mr. Smith need to learn that he died like Mr. Hartwick in Chapter Five?

16) The Old Town Hall ~ When Darlene Wilson first opened her photography studio in the old town hall, she felt a man's presence. She said, "It's not frightening, but I'm certain he doesn't approve of women working late. He becomes more intrusive as the evening wanes. As if he wants to let me know I should be home with

my family." One night Darlene was so immersed in her work that she missed his subtle signals, so he took a more direct approach. He appeared on top of the garret-like skylight that is above her desk. Upon seeing his eerie face looming down at her, do you think she left? You bet she did!

17) The 1870 Amity Parsonage ~ There is a quaint, yellow Victorian out on Newport Bridge Road in Amity that could turn anyone into an old-house lover. It hints of leisure, summer afternoons spent rocking in wicker chairs on the front porch while sipping mint juleps. Kim and John Starks bought the parsonage in November of 1988. Their son, Ryan, was born one month later. It wasn't long before Ryan let Kim know he was terrified of the bathroom on the second floor. From his infant tub he'd stare past her into the wavy glass mirror over the sink and scream and cry. He became so inconsolable whenever he was in that bathroom that Kim had to bathe him in the kitchen.

Months later a friend from college visited. After using the bathroom, she said, "I feel something in your bathroom. I think you have a ghost." The Stark's bathroom continued to pulsate with an ominous energy until it was updated in 1992.

18) Over thirty years ago a New Jersey couple phoned Raynor Realty to inquire about a magnificent farm out on Jessup Road. It consisted of a three-story colonial farmhouse, a huge dairy barn and several out buildings on a large amount of acreage. As soon as realtor Barbara White showed the couple their find, they said they'd take it. They must have been awfully smitten, because they were caught robbing the Ramsey National Bank for the down payment. A trial took

place with Jane Gilman as their attorney. Gilman was so intrigued by their O'Henrian story that when her clients were incarcerated she bought the farm herself. It wasn't long before she realized the house had another tale — it was haunted. Jane held séances from time to time to communicate with its spirits. One night she invited Barbara White and eleven other villagers. The ghost did indeed join them. He presented himself by making rattling noises and moving the empty chair saved for his occupancy. When the one non-believer among them scoffed at the happenings, the ghost went silent. Moral: Don't invite a non-believer to your next séance. He'll be nothing but a wet blanket.

19) Arlene's Gift Shop ~ Arlene and David Hedgecock bought one of Sugar Loaf's colonial buildings on Main Street in 1998. It dates back to the late 1700s and was once used as a rooming house. Shortly after they began to remodel, they realized they had an aberration. Every afternoon at four thirty and every evening at eight a shadow walked across the front hall and climbed the staircase. Arlene has also felt someone invisible stroke her hair on more than one occasion. She even has been rudely yanked from a deep sleep by a ghostly prod. To this day a shadow can be seen making his daily afternoon and evening rounds.

20) The Parker House ~ There is a 200-year-old colonial on the edge of Sugar Loaf that sends chills up the spines of anyone who passes. Several years ago a family by the name of Parker lived there. They confided in friends that they heard nightly disturbances in their attic and were quite sure they had a ghost. Then their luck turned from bad to tragic. When

they lost their son in a dreadful car accident, they decided the house held too many memories and moved. The scuttlebutt in the village claims one of the many owners to have lived there since had a tree fall through the roof of their children's bedroom. Could a spirit be so powerful that it could veer harm toward children? We can only hope not.

21) Annie's Gift ~ Deidre Hamling of Four Corners Road encountered a psychic manifestation that she is forever grateful for. In 1966 she visited her parents at their summer home in Lavallette, New Jersey. She was pregnant with her second child and went to take a nap in the guest room that had formerly belonged to her grandmother, Annie. When she lay down on Annie's bed, she became overcome with emotion and sobbed into the pillow. Deirdre missed her grandmother and wished she were alive to meet her children. She prayed, "Annie please give me a sign that you are with us from time to time." Suddenly she heard a voice in her head say, "Open the drawer, open the drawer!" She reached over and opened the night table drawer that separated the twin beds. There on top lay a card from her grandmother. It had been written to her mother over twenty-five years earlier. The sentiment was a prayer entitled, "Trust in the Master Weaver." Its message was to accept that we are only here for a short time before we must go back to join God in the spirit world. Deirdre was certain that her prayer was answered. Finding the card was like receiving one of Annie's gentle kisses on her forehead. Too excited to sleep, she showed her mother the card. Her mother was as astonished as she was. She said, "I haven't seen that card in years. I go into that drawer all the time and it has never been there."

22) The first time Susan Rockwell and her family walked into their new colonial on Newport Bridge Road, Susan saw the apparition of a woman with long, dark, wavy hair in a high-collared, white blouse and a long, tan skirt fleeing down the stairs in a panic. Since then, she has seen this poor woman reenact this scene dozens of times. Susan has delved into her land's history and learned that a farmhouse inhabited the very spot where her house now stands. The former house burned to the ground and a young woman is said to have perished in the fire.

23) Who better than one of our librarians to tell a ghost story? Shortly after Kathleen Georgalas and her family moved from Minneapolis to Warwick in 1996 something mind-boggling happened. She, like so many others, was not a believer. Yet once settled in her and her family's new bi-level out on Jones Road she was awakened by an eerie sight. It was the middle of the night when she spied a vaporous gentleman about six feet tall with blondish-gray hair wearing blue jeans and a dark, plaid flannel shirt standing at the edge of her bed. Oddly, he stood with his back to her. As she spotted him, he looked at her over his left shoulder. When he seemed to realize she was behind him he looked as startled as she did. Kathleen immediately shook her husband Artie awake. Of course, as soon as he awakened the vision was gone. Barely dismayed Artie murmured, "You must have been dreaming," and fell back to sleep. Little did he know that just one month later their youngest son, Thomas, would wake them in the middle of the night, looking pale and shaken. "There's a man in my room staring at me," he insisted. "What does he look like?" asked his mother. "He's wearing blue jeans and a plaid shirt and has gray hair."

Could this man be the farmer who used to own most of Jones Road? This is definitely a question for our Bill Raynor.

24) Shortly after Sheila and James Scheuermann moved into their Victorian home on Wheeler Avenue, their precocious sixteen-month-old Peter started to talk about "da lady." He would say, "I can't go upstairs, da lady is up there," or "Look, there's da lady." Not enough to suspect a ghost you scoff. What about the phantom footsteps, odors and the recurring appearance of hairpins? The busy couple frequently smelled cinnamon buns baking in the morning while they hurried to leave for work. They rarely ate breakfast and certainly didn't have time to bake. Sheila wore her hair short and never used hairpins, yet they constantly clinked in her vacuum. While nestled in their bed, she and James frequently witnessed the sound of footfalls slowly descending the stairs. They later learned that the house was once owned by sisters, Carie Knapp and Lois Dalade. Carie is remembered by many for her marvelous baking and Lois — could she have been "da lady?"

25) Instead of anxiety, Cass felt like she was going home the day she interviewed for her job as bookkeeper. And understandably so — the office building where she was about to work for the next eighteen years was converted from a Victorian house on Oakland Avenue that she knew well. It was the house that had once belonged to her great-grandparents. She remembered going there every Sunday as a child. Perhaps that's why she witnessed the flurry of supernatural activity that frequented the building. When Cass walked by the bathroom on the first floor, water would blast into the sink. Whenever she worked late, she heard someone pacing the second floor above her. Years later,

when her office was moved upstairs, she saw the attic door hook lift ever so slowly out of its eye and spin to an unlatched position. Cass was certain that the person on the other side of that door meant no harm. The ghostly childish pranks even amused her. One warm April night she worked overtime by herself until after midnight. Dark figures flitted into her peripheral vision. But with deadlines hanging over her, she was too busy to feel spooked. Until she took a break. When she opened the window to smoke a cigarette, the entity became more personal. In a woman's voice it whispered, "Cassandra Ann." Only her great-grandmother used her full name when she addressed her.

AFTERWORD

Haunted or not, the Warwick Valley in Orange County, New York, is a very special place. It is renowned for its bucolic setting dotted with dairy farms, apple orchards, elegant Victorians, and charming farmhouses. Some people have remarked that the valley possesses a spiritual energy that easily draws people in the arts and different religious groups to its rolling hills. Perhaps that is why some of its residents are reluctant to leave, even after they have died.

Again, I want to thank every person who took the time to share his or her ghostly encounter with me. I respect and believe every one of you.

Donna Reis

AUTHOR'S ADVICE

Interviewing Ghosts

First you need to let go
of the idea that they are enlightened.
Unfortunately all those times
you held your tongue
certain that the person before you
would get his in the afterlife
were in vain. Truth be known,
some specters are as nasty
after death as they were before.
Second, try not to fall for their stories
of how they funneled from their bodies
in a vaporous swirl,
how they chose
not to cross the amber river
because of some dangling injustice,
some unresolved mystery.
And don't be swayed by the age-old excuse
that they didn't know they were dead.

Try not to be impressed
by their translucent togas
that glow like a heavenly-lit-scrim.
This outfit is merely worn
to wake you at three in the morning
to give weight to a last goodbye,
an unearthly warning
or the more violent shaking of chains.
Remember that they never use doorways,
yet they always take the stairs.
When they are feeling particularly dramatic
they curl through walls like smoke
or swoop up behind you as a bodiless head,
rudely release an effluvious odor,
a maniacal laugh.
And most important, don't count on them
for anything practical such as reminding
you where you left your keys
because they are undoubtedly the ones who hid them.

Warwick

May blessings be about you; beautiful vale of Warwick;
may your fields and forests be as green, your waters
as bright, the cattle on your hundred hills as fruitful
as in the days of old, when my yet youthful foot
pressed their greensward, my youthful lungs drew life
from the inspiration of your clear mountain breezes.
May independence, innocence and plenty be the
inheritance of your sons, the dowry of your daughters;
… may you be, as nature only can, of all the works
of God, forever beautiful, unchanged and young; and
so farewell fair vale of Warwick.

Frank Forester
1807-1858

ABOUT THE ARTISTS

Christine Cole is a working artist in the Champlain Valley of Vermont. Her paintings and drawings have been exhibited in galleries throughout New England. She has lived in the Warwick Valley and holds fond memories of cherished haunts. She currently resides in an old brick house in Burlington with a friendly spirit or two.

Cover artist Shotsie Gorman is a painter, poet, sculptor, and one of the world's most renowned tattoo artists. His art works, furniture, handmade boxes, and carpet and tile designs have been sought by galleries around the world. He was the publisher and editor of the former "Tattoo Advocate Journal." His first book of poetry, *The Black Marks He Made*, was published by Proteus Press, together with a companion spoken-word CD produced by Record Plant, Inc. (1999). His writing has placed as a finalist (2001) and second place winner (1998) in the Allen Ginsberg Competition sponsored by Passaic County Community College and the New Jersey Council on the Arts. Shotsie currently lives in Warwick, New York, with Kristine Sicoli and his children, Lucas Orion and Emma Fairchild.